*Why Jews Do
What They Do:
The History of
Jewish Customs
throughout the Cycle
of the Jewish Year*

by Daniel Sperber

translated by Yaakov Elman

Ktav Publishing House, Inc.
Hoboken, N.J. 07030

Library of Congress Cataloging-in-Publication Data

Sperber, Daniel.
    (Minhage Yisra'el. English)
        Why Jews do what they do : the History of Jewish customs
    throughout the cycle of the Jewish year / by Daniel Sperber ;
    translated by Yaakov Elman.
            p.   cm.
    Includes bibliographical references.
    ISBN 0-88125-604–8
    1. Judaism–Customs and practices. 2. Fasts and feasts–Judaism.
I. Title.
BM700 .S63513 1999
296.4 '3 ..ddc21   98-55104
                                                                  CIP

Manufactured in the United States
Distributed by
KTAV Publishing House, Inc.
900 Jefferson St.
Hoboken , NJ 07030

Table of Contents

INTRODUCTION 1

PART I — SHABBAT

CHAPTER 1 12
Reciting Mizmor Shir le-Yom ha-Shabbat Twice

CHAPTER 2 22
Mizmor le-Todah During Kabbalat Shabbat

CHAPTER 3 27
Regarding Kiddush

CHAPTER 4 43
Kiddush During Seudah Shelishit

PART II — PASSOVER

CHAPTER 5 51
Shemurah Matzah from the Time of Reaping

PART III — MINOR OCCASIONS

CHAPTER 6 73
Taanit Bahab

PART IV — SEFIRAH

CHAPTER 7 82
"Leshem Yihud" Before Counting the Omer

CHAPTER 8 86
The Customs of Mourning During
the Counting of the Omer

CHAPTER 9 102
Sephardic Customs Regarding Hair-Cutting
During Sefirah

PART V — SHAVUOT

CHAPTER 10 112
Spreading Grasses in Synagogues on Shavuot

PART VI — THE THREE WEEKS

CHAPTER 11 117
The Dispute Over Announcing a Fast

CHAPTER 12 128
The Prohibition of Eating Meat and Drinking
Wine During the Three Weeks

PART VII — ROSH HASHANAH

CHAPTER 13 141
Vetotzi le-or mishpateinu
ha-yom/Ayom-Kadosh

CHAPTER 14 150
One Hundred Teqiot

CHAPTER 15 153
The Prohibition of Eating Nuts on
Rosh Hashanah

CHAPTER 16 167
Oseh Ha-Shalom

PART VIII — YOM KIPPUR

CHAPTER 17 172
Three Tevilot on Erev Yom Kippur

PART IX — SUKKOT

CHAPTER 18 177
Birkat ha-Haftarah on Hol ha-Moed Sukkot

CHAPTER 19 182
Regarding the Crowns of the Torah Scrolls
on Simhat Torah

CHAPTER 20 187
The Hadar in the Hadran

CHAPTER 21 191
Hatan ha-Torah—Hatam Torah

CHAPTER 22 ··194
The Haftarah of Simhat Torah

PART X — HANNUKAH

CHAPTER 23 ··202
Ha-Nerot Halalu

CHAPTER 24 ··213
Kindling Hannukah Lights According to
the Custom of the Jews of Persia

CHAPTER 25 ··216
The Parshiyot of Sheqalim, Zahkhor, and
Hahodesh, According to the Custom of
Eretz Israel

Introduction

RESEARCH REGARDING CUSTOMS is an area of scholarship which is still in its infancy. This is not to say that many large and important works have not been written in this area.[1] On the contrary, much spadework has been done in gathering and classifying customs, and in uncovering their origins and reasons.[2] Various geographical and cultural regions and particular historical periods have been studied from this point of view; various scholars have even begun the work of understanding the special characteristics of each of these regions and eras.[3] The same is true in regard to particular customs, whose development has been well described.[4] Likewise, complexes of customs, such as customs connected with time-bound mitzvot (Shabbat, holidays, fasts)[5] or particular halakhic areas (such as the halakhot of mourning),[6] have merited comprehensive studies. Indeed, a vast and ramified literature which includes a variety of viewpoints and methodologies exists. Nevertheless, despite all this, the essen-

1

tial foundation necessary for a profound understanding of this branch of study has not yet been laid. For example, a complete catalogue of all the customs of every Jewish community has not been established.[7] Moreover, basic questions regarding the organization and arrangement of this sort of material have not yet even been raised. No one has proposed a unified method of cataloguing, methods of cross-referencing, etc. Should the material be arranged according to halakhic categories (as, for example, in the order of the Shulhan Arukh), or perhaps according to country and region, or by era? No opinion has yet been offered regarding all these matters, nor have methods of categorization and numbering for this sort of material been suggested, as has long been the case for folklore studies. There is no full bibliography of *minhag*-books—small pamphlets that have been preserved in imperfect condition,[8] although there is now a partial bibliography on studies of *minhagim*.[9] Likewise, there is no bibliography listing all siddurim and *mahzorim*, both in print and in manuscript. However, recently we have been enriched with a bibliography of studies related to all aspects of Jewish prayer.[10] Much important material, regarding which there is no precise knowledge, remains hidden in libraries and private collections.

In the absence of such basic tools of scholarship, whoever wishes to involve himself in this area of research must forge his own path, his own methods of work—area studies, diachronic regarding details or from a wider perspective, etc. The many and scattered fruits

of these studies constitute only a handful in any particular area, and thus do not provide a full and continuous picture. In contrast to the study of folklore, there are still no generally accepted premises, as noted above.
Therefore, when I first decided to gather and arrange my writings, published and unpublished, on this subject, the method of arrangement and organization of the material was not clear to me. In the end, after no little consideration, I chose to follow the easiest and most generally agreed upon path—i.e., to follow the order of the Shulhan Arukh, more or less, at least for the first volume of what has now become a series of six volumes. I could have classified and arranged the material another way, according to particular categories, such as customs which were created as halakhic compromises (see, for example, vol. 2, chap. 2), or because of a lack of clear understanding of the halakhic sources,[11] customs whose development depended on historical events,[12] or local conditions,[13] strange customs,[14] customs which originated under the influence of superstitious beliefs, customs which concern numbers or are connected with kabbalistic numerology,[15] or the various types of customs arising out of error.[16] Likewise, I could have composed a chapter unto itself on customs which came into being because of the struggle against the Karaites.[17] However, as noted, I initially decided in favor of the generally accepted method of following the arrangement of the Shulhan Arukh, which would be easiest for most readers. At times I have only lightly touched on matters

which really deserve treatment on their own, as, for
example, the manner of transmittal of customs and the
development of *minhag*-collections,[18] and likewise the
topic of the creation of new customs and the spread of
minhagim. An extremely interesting additional topic
which deserves attention is how customs are reflected in
Jewish art, as in the illustrations accompanying manuscripts and the like.[19] I hope that this book will open a
small window onto a large hall, through which others
may glance, be entranced by the light, and provide still
more light for others.

Notes

1. The reader will find a well-organized, comprehensive
introduction to this subject in M. Elon's great work, *Jewish
Law: History, Sources, Principles*, Philadelphia, 1993, pp.
67–713. And so too in J. Roth, *The Halakhic Process: A Sys-
temic Analysis* (New York, 1986), pp. 205–231. See also the
comments of I. Twersky, in his *Introduction to the Code of
Maimonides* (New Haven, 1980), pp. 124–134, and his *Rabad
of Posquières* (New York, 1980), pp. 241–242.

2. See H. C. Dobrinsky, *A Treasury of Sephardic Laws and Cus-
toms* (Hoboken: Ktav, 1986); H. J. Zimmels, *Ashkenazim and
Sepharadim*, reprint ed. (Hoboken: Ktav, 1996); Y. D. Eisen-
stein, *Otzar ha-Dinim veha-Minhagim* (New York, 5677); G.
Felder, *Yesodei Yeshurun*, 2 vols. (Jerusalem, 5741); Y. H.
Friedman, *Liqqutei Maharih*, 3 vols., reprint ed. (Jerusalem,
5725); S. T. Gaguine, *Keter Shem Tov*, 6 pts. (London and
Jerusalem, 5694–5741); A. E. Hirchowitz, *Otzar Kol Min-
hagei Yeshurun*, reprint ed. (Jerusalem, 5730); A. I. Sperling,
Taamei ha-Minhagim u-Meqorei ha-Dinim, expanded ed.
(Jerusalem, 5721).

INTRODUCTION

3. Recently there has been an increased interest in Ashkenazi customs. See Y. A. Dinari, *Hakhmei Ashkenaz be-Shilhei Yemei ha-Beinayim: Darkeihem ve-Kitveihem ba-Halakhah* (Jerusalem, 5744), and see his excellent bibliography on pp. 190–228; I. M. Ta-Shema, *Minhag Ashkenaz ha-Qadmon* (Jerusalem, 1992); idem, *Halakha, Minhag u-Meziut be-Ashkenaz, 1350-1500,* (Jerusalem, 1966); B. S. Hamburger, *Shoshanei Minhag Ashkenaz* (Benei Brak, 1995); and Y. (E.) Zimmer, *Olam ke-Minhago Noheg* (Jerusalem, 1996).

4. See Y. L. Zlotnick, "Me-Aggadot ha-Shabbat u-Minhageha, *Sinai* 25 (5709): 5–31, and 28 (5711): 55–68, 330–348, on Yahrzeit; Y. Avida, *Koso shel Eliyahu: Naftulei ha-Minhag be-Hitraqmuto* (Jerusalem, 5718), A. Yaari, *Kiryat Sefer* vol. 33 (5718): 118–130, 233–250, and 36 (5721): 103–118, on "Mi Sheberakh."

5. See, for example, the large compendium by A. Yaari, *Toledot Hag Simhat Torah* (Jerusalem, 5724); so too R. Y. Kohen's article, "Seder Kabbalat Shabbat u-Pizmon Lekha Dodi," in *Mekorot u-Mesorot* (Jerusalem, 5742), pp. 74–106; and add to it, H. Leshem, *Shabbat u-Moadei Yisrael*, vol. 1 (Tel Aviv, 5725), pp. 13–18, as well as "Minhagei Shovavim bi-Tefutzot Yisrael, ibid., pp. 107–129; R. Yaakov Werdiger, *Sefer Edut le-Yisrael* (Bnei Brak, 1968) (on marriage, circumcision, *pidyon ha-ben*, etc.); idem, *Ner Shabbat* (Tel Aviv, n.d.); M. Benayahu, *Sefer Yom Tov Sheni shel Galuyot* (Jerusalem, 5747); Y. Rivkind, *Le-Ot ule-Zikaron: Toledot Bar Mitzvah*, etc. (New York, 5702, etc.).

6. See, for example, M. Benayahu's extensive study of *maamadot* and *moshavot* in *Sefer Zikaron leha-Rav Yitzhak Nissim, z.t.l. . . .,* under his editorship (Jerusalem, 5745), and in the doctoral dissertation of Nisan Rubin, "Al Hilkhot Avelut" (Ramat Gan University). And see his articles in *Bar-Ilan* 10 (5732): 111–122, and in *Sefer Zikaron le-Avraham Spiegelman* (5739), pp. 135–144; S. Glick, *Or le-Aval* (Efrat, 1991); idem.

5

Or ve-Nihumim (Efrat, 1993); idem, *Or Noga Aleihem* (Efrat, 1997). My student, Dr. Hayyim Talbi, has composed a comprehensive master's thesis, as yet unpublished, on mourning customs.

7. In the meantime, see most recently S. P. Gelbard, *Otzar Taamei ha-Minhagim* (Petah Tikvah, 1995). There are *minhagim* which have been completely forgotten, and it is incumbent on us to rescue them from neglect. I would like to emphasize one example of this from Masekhet Derekh Eretz Zuta 7:3 (in my edition [Jerusalem, 5742], pp. 49–50). "Just as a bride, when in her father's house, behaves modestly, but when she leaves displays herself, and says: Whoever has something to testify regarding me should come and testify, etc." This indicates that at the time of marriage the bride would prove that she was a virgin so as to receive her *ketubbah* as a virgin. Such a custom of bringing proof of virginity after the marriage's consummation is known among many peoples, and among Jews as well (see, for example, *Qorot Lub ve-Yahadutah . . .* , ed. A. Goldberg [Jerusalem, 5742], n. 89, pp. 277–278; A. Brauer, *Yehudei Kurdistan* [Jerusalem, 5708], p. 116, etc.), but not from Talmudic sources (see *Encyclopaedia Judaica*, vol. 11, col. 1045). Note the following example in the *piyyut* of the Byzantine *payyatan* from Italy, Amitai, who lived in Oria and died in 886. In his Kedushta for a bridegroom he writes, "And how pleasant is it for the bridegroom on the day of his wedding to display the purity of the tokens of virginity of his wife with head held high" (see *Megilat Ahimaaz*, ed. Klar [Jerusalem, 5734], p. 94, and Yonah David's edition of Amitai's poetry published in 1985, p. 23, and see Klar's note on p. 169.) Only after this does he state, "For witnesses to sign the marriage contract, and his joy complete." Only after the proof of virginity has been displayed do the witnesses sign the marriage contract, after it is clear

to them that the bride does merit a virgin's portion (= 200 zuz). This is a startling innovation (see E. Fleischer's comment in *Hasafrut* 30–31 [1981]: 14, and that of Y. Ta-Shema in *Sidra* 3 [5747]: 111, n. 50). Since we know of the close ties between the teachings of the early Italian *payyatanim* and Eretz Yisrael (see Fleischer, op. cit., pp. 131 f., and esp. 141 f.), the idea may seriously be considered that this custom reflects a similar one found in the Eretz Yisrael version of Derekh Eretz Zuta. Thus, to compile a full list of customs we must uncover forgotten sources.

Likewise, we must take into account the customs of various communities according to type, origin, and authoritative source, and compare them to similar ones elsewhere. For example, in *Sefer Noheg be-Hokhmah* by R. Yosef Ben Naim (a Moroccan scholar, 1892–1961), ed. R. Moshe Amar (Israel, 5747), p. 27, it is stated: "And so they store cakes from Passover to Shavuot, and eat them for breakfast on Shavuot." Compare the booklet *Sarid u-Palit* I, by R. Y. H. Toledano (n.d.), p. 8, who cites "a fragment of the prayers of Rabbi Maimon, father of the Rambam," in the translation of R. David Ha-Sab'oni. (There were two scholars by that name, one died in 1611 and one in 1733; see R. Yaakov Moshe Toledano, *Ner Hamaarav* [Jerusalem, 5671], pp. 108, 157. We refer here to the second of them. My thanks to Dr. Moshe Amar for clarifying this for me.) In an addition to this fragment by the translator it is stated, "And so they store cakes from Passover to Shavuot, and eat them for breakfast on Shavuot." (See also *Zemanim* by R. M. Y. Zaks [Jerusalem, 5710], p 51. On pp. 50–51 he notes the custom of throwing apples from the roof of the synagogue on Shavuot, cited by R. D. Ha-Sab'oni there. The source for this custom is the Targum Sheni to Esther, chap. 3, and we shall discuss this elsewhere.)

The work needed is tremendous, stretching across the

whole gamut of halakhic literature in print and in manuscript, and must be based on the testimonies of the senior scholars of each community.

8. See P. Y. Cohen, *Otzar ha-Be'urim veha-Perushim* (London, 5712), pp. 467–475, where he lists books devoted to customs and enactments. See also R. Sh. Deblitzki, "Reshimat Sifrei Minhagim (Mabat me-Rabbim)," *Tagim* 2–3 (5732): 104–108. On Ashkenazic books on customs, see Dinari (n. 2 above), pp. 345–346. The bibliography of A. S. Freidus is worthy of note, in *Studies in Jewish Bibliography and Related Subjects in Memory of Abraham Solomon Freidus (1867–1923)* (New York, 1929), pp. lxviii–cxxx, "Jewish Customs." (My thanks to Prof. Y. Ta-Shema for turning my attention to this important list.)

Here is the place to thank Machon Yerushalayim for its initiative in publishing the series "Mif'al Torat Hakhmei Ashkenaz," under whose aegis several basic *sifrei minhagim* have been published, among them *Minhagei Mahrash Neustadt, Minhagei R. Avraham Klausner,* R. Isaac Tyrnau, *Minhagei Kehillat Worms,* etc. See the review by Y. Yuval, *Kiryat Sefer* 61 (5746–47): 349–359.

9. See *Minhagei Yisrael*, vol. 5 (Jerusalem, 1995), pp. 217–309, by my good friends, Dr. Meir Refeld and Rabbi Prof. J. Tabory.

10. That of Rabbi Prof. J. Tabory, *Supplement to Kiryat Sefer* 64 (1992–93), parts of which had already appeared in *Areshet* 4 (5744): 101–112, and 5 (5745): 85–112. See also the special lists by R. Hayyim Kraus in *Otzrot Yerushalayim,* pt. 240 (5739) ("Birkhot ha-Hayyim"), pp. 5639–5640, and likewise pt. 640 (5739), pp. 756-762; so too M. Halamish's articles in *Asufot* 1 (5747): 361–377 and 2 (5748): 191–200. It appears that the subject catalogue of the National Library in Jerusalem is the most complete listing of editions of siddurim and *mahzorim.*

11. To this category belong all twenty-four fast-days which are

enumerated in Megillat Taanit Batra (see *Minhagei Yisrael* [Hebrew ed.], vol. 1, chap. 25, regarding the matter of fasting on Rosh Hodesh); and regarding the fast of the Ninth of Av, see the wonderful article by R. S. Z. Leiman in *Jewish Quarterly Review* 74 (1983): 185–195. Likewise, regarding the "Purims" of various communities (see, for example, R. Hayyim Palaggi, *Mo'ed le-Khol Hai*, siman 6, p. 36b; and *Responsa Hatam Sofer*, O.H. 191). See also *Responsa Havvot Yair* 138; A. Danon, *REJ* 54, 1907, pp. 113–137.

12. See the classic study by Jacob Katz, "Ma'ariv bi-Zmano ve-she-lo bi-Zmano–Dugma le-Ziqqah bein Minhag Halakhah ve-Hevrah," *Zion* 35 (5730): 35–60 (= Y. Katz, *Halakhah be-Qabbalah* [Jerusalem, 5744], pp. 175–200); add to this the discussion in *Minhagim de-Kehila Kadisha Vermaizah* (= Worms), ed. Hamburger and Zimmer (Jerusalem, 5748), pp. 107–109, n. 2; Y. Ta-Shema in *Tarbiz* 45 (5736): 128–137, and 52 (5743): 309–323; Y. Zimmer in *Sinai* 73 (5733): 252–264 regarding the mitzvah of sukkah on Shemini Atzeret in the communities of Ashkenaz. Finally, see I. Ta-Shema in *Sidra* 3 (5747): 157–158.

13. See for example the discussion of the custom of using apples on Shavuot, R. M.Y.Z. Zaks, *Zemanim*, Jerusalem, 5711, pp. 50f, and in *Minhagei Yisrael* vol. 6.

14. Regarding the customs of Hoshana Rabbah, in particular the examination of one's shadow in the light of the moon in order to determine whether one's body is whole or missing a head or other limbs, see *Kaf ha-Hayyim*, O.H. 684:19, and ibid., 3, Ramban to Numbers 14:9 (cited in *Matteh Moshe* 957); *Sefer Hasidim*, ed. Wistenetzki, 1144, pp. 378–379; and *Minhagei Yisrael*, vol. 6.

15. See below, chaps. 2, 3, 7, 14, 15, 16, 17, 23, and see Y. Ta-Shema, *Tarbiz* 39 (5730): 184–194, on reciting "E-l Melekh Ne'eman" in order to make up the number of 248 words in Keriat Shema, corresponding to the number of

limbs in one's body (*Shibbolei ha-Leqet*, siman 15, ed. Mirsky, pp. 171–175), and the comments of Sh. Z. Havlin, *Tarbiz* 40 (5731): 107–109. The practice of counting words and interpreting the number symbolism was greatly developed by the Hasidei Ashkenaz; see *Sefer ha-Roqe'ah, Siddur R. Shlomo mi-Germaiza*, ed. Hirschler (Jerusalem, 5732). See *Minhagei Yisrael* vol. 2 (1991), pp. 159–182.

See also *Shulhan Arukh* O.H. 271 (Rema), regarding adding the words יום השישי in order to make up the number of 72 words, corresponding to the number of letters in the Shem Hameforash, and note the words of the Tur in O.H. 113: "According to my brother, R. Yehiel, ז'ל, "those who interpreted hints (דורשי רשומות) are the Hasidei Ashkenaz, who would weigh and count the number of words of the prayers and blessings, and the reasons for their composition in this way." A similar comment, without the reference to Hasidei Ashkenaz, may be found in *Responsa Rashba* 4:20. However, note the critical remarks of the Avudraham (Abudarham), cited in *Beit Yosef* O.H. 113: "There are those who counted the words in every blessing of the Shemoneh Esreh, and cited biblical verses for each one, where the letters in the verse correspond to the number of the words in each blessing. And so was my practice at first, but after that it seemed to me that there is no basis for this at all, for there is no place in the world where everyone recites the Shemoneh Esreh in exactly the same way, word for word. Rather, some add words and some delete, and so the count is not uniform and makes no difference, except for the one who actually makes the count and proposed the interpretation, but not for anyone else; why then should we burden those who would make such counts to write them?"

In general, see Yaakov Katz, *Halakhah ve-Kabbalah* (Jerusalem, 5744), as well as the article by Y. Benayahu in *Daat* 5 (5740): 61–115, and that by Y. Halamish in *Daat* 21

(5748): 85–102, and in *Minhagei Yisrael* vol. 3 (1994), pp. 113–172.

16. See *Minhagei Yisrael*, vol. 1 (Hebrew ed.), pp. 31–38, on the authority of a custom, and vol. 2, pp. 76–125, on mistaken customs.

17. For example, see R. M. M. Kasher, *Torah Shelemah*, Beshallah, pt. 21, pp. 332–333, regarding the placing of a knife on the Sabbath table (but see J. Trachtenberg, *Jewish Magic and Superstition*, p. 299 n. 5), and likewise Y. Gartner, *Hadarom* 36 (Tishrei 5733): 125–162, *Milet* 2 (5744): 201–224, *Bar Ilan* 20–21 (5743): 128–44, *Sinai* 89 (5741): 157–164, and now in his *Gilgulei Minhag be-Olam ha-Halakhah* (Jerusalem, 1995).

18. See below, chap. 16, on the blessing for the Haftarah for Hol ha-Moed Sukkot, and chap. 12, on the prohibition of eating meat or drinking wine during the Three Weeks, where we found a source which cites two separate traditions. This phenomenon teaches us much about the way these collectors did their work, more as collectors than as critical sifters.

19. For now see what I wrote in *Bibliotheca Orientalis* 41 (1984): 158–168, and in *Minhagei Yisrael*, vols. 4 and 5; and see the excellent articles by E. Horowitz in *Jewish History* 1 (1986): 75–90 and *Kiryat Sefer* 63 (5746–48): 583–586. Vol. 6 of *Minhagei Yisrael* deals with this subject at length, as do chaps. 16–20 of vol. 4 (pp. 78–184).

PART I
SHABBAT

CHAPTER 1[1]
Reciting Mizmor Shir le-Yom ha-Shabbat Twice

AN INTERESTING EXPLANATION for the custom in Prague of reciting Psalm 92 twice during Kabbalat Shabbat connects it with the Maharal of Prague's golem. The story goes that one Erev Shabbat the golem ran amok and the inhabitants of Prague could not calm him down or stop him. The Maharal was called to help; when he removed the Ineffable Name from around his neck, the golem fell lifeless before them. Since this occurred after the community had recited Mizmor Shir le-Yom ha-Shabbat, they were concerned that the Maharal had violated the

Sabbath by "taking a soul," and so when the Maharal returned to the Altneuschul, they recited the mizmor again in order to make it plain that the Maharal had done what he had done *before the Sabbath had come in*. As a memorial of this event, the custom of reciting the mizmor twice was adopted.[2]

First of all, we must dispose of the Maharal's golem, since it never existed, and was a creation of the nineteenth century. The source for the story of the Maharal's golem is a volume called *Niflaot Maharal*, published in St. Petersburg in 5669, and purported to be by R. Yitzhak Katz, the Maharal's son-in-law. Already in 5670 R. M. M. Eckstein cast doubt on the authenticity of this book in the introduction to his *Sefer Yetzirah*, published in Siget.

> It is now half a year since I heard of a manuscript of the Gaon R. Yitzhak, the son-in-law of the Maharal of Prague, in the library in Mainz, in which is recounted the signs and wonders that the Gaon, the Maharal performed in creating a golem in order to protect the Jews of Prague from blood libels. I was very happy to hear this news, but when I went through the book from start to finish I found a number of grievous errors, things which were against the works of the Rishonim and Aharonim and Halakhah, and [so] this must all be *falsehood and lies*—there is no manuscript and no signs and wonders, but there is a *golem* [= a fool],[3] and it is shameful enough in our day to seek lies and falsehoods and to publish them in Israel, attributing them to a great person.

Among other things, R. Eckstein caught the forger in several anachronisms, such as confusing R. Yaakov Ginzburg of Friedberg with his cousin, R. Hayyim b. R. Bezalel, the brother of the Maharal; it was the latter who served as Rav in Friedberg. More than that, as R. Eckstein pointed out, how could R. Katz have referred to R. Ginzburg as the teacher of the author of the *Tosafot Yom Tov* when it had not been published in his lifetime![4]

Thus any explanation of this custom which connects it with the golem must be false, and we must look elsewhere to understand why the mizmor was recited twice in the Altneuschul in Prague.

According to the Arizal's custom, Kabbalat Shabbat was performed twice, once in the fields and once in the house. In the fields they would recite Mizmor Havu la-Shem Benei Elim (Psalms 29) in fear and trembling, followed by Lekha Dodi three times, and then Mizmor Shir le-Yom ha-Shabbat and Ha-Shem Malakh Ge'ut Lavesh (Psalms 93). Returning home, they would put on their *taleitim*, walk several times around the table, which was set for the Shabbat meal, and repeat what they had said in the fields, including Mizmor Shir le-Yom ha-Shabbat, "for there in the field they had only done a *tikkun* of outside forces from the aspect of the Inner Light, and now the *tikkun* was to ascend from the aspect of the Surrounding Light."[5]

Now, in the Arizal's time they did indeed go out into the fields outside the town, deriving this custom from Shabbat 119a: "R. Hanina would wrap himself [in his *talit*][6] and stand up at the evening of Erev Shabbat and say: 'Come, *let us go* toward the Sabbath Queen." "For if it were as some lightheaded people think, that it is sufficient to accept the Sabbath in their own courtyard, [R. Hanina] would not have had to say 'let us go out.' Apparently, they were in the middle of the city and would gather together to go out to the fields to greet the Sabbath, the honored guest."[7]

However, in his *Seder ha-Yom*,[8] R. Moshe Ibn Makhir rules that it is sufficient to go out to a garden or courtyard, "a place free [of bustle] and proper for accepting [Shabbat], but one is not obligated to go out of the city. [But] all is according to the person and the place."

Siddur ha-Shelah also casts doubt on the need to leave the city; "in conclusion, it seems to me that one who leaves the city in order to accept the Sabbath is not one of the pious but rather one of those who arouse wonderment! . . . It is better to accept the Shabbat in the synagogue."[9] The same sentiment is expressed earlier in *Yosef Ometz*, whose author hailed from Frankfurt.

> It is not my custom to recite the first stanza of Lekha Dodi in Kabbalat Shabbat [לקראת שבת לכו ונלכה] because *we are not accustomed to go from place to place* [i.e., outside the town] in order to greet the Sabbath, as is the custom in Eretz Yisrael, or at least to go out to the courtyard of the synagogue, as the *Seder ha-Yom* points out at length. . . . Rather I say לבבתני שבת מלכה in its place, in order to fill in the

lamed stanza of the signature of the composer of this prayer.[10]

Clearly, the custom of the Arizal was not accepted in its original form, since it caused too much hardship for those who lived in large cities, or for the old, for whom it was difficult to walk long distances or to climb in fields or hills. Even where the synagogue held a large congregation, it would have been difficult for all of them to exit as a body to leave the city and return for Maariv.[11]

No matter how far the congregants went, even to the synagogue courtyard, it would have been possible for them to recite Mizmor Shir le-Yom ha-Shabbat twice, as the Arizal laid down. However, in places where this custom was not practiced, there was no need for the twofold recitation. However, there was an intermediate custom, where the mizmor was said once, after which the congregants went into the courtyard and recited Bameh Madlikin, after which they recited the mizmor a second time.[12] In this way they shortened the second recitation of the Kabbalat Shabbat service, as described in *Sefer ha-Kavvanot*, cited above—a doubly long version which would have been a hardship for the congregation.

Thus, the recitation of Bameh Madlikin served to separate the twin recitations of the mizmor, and in this way it is possible to explain this custom even when the entire Kabbalat Shabbat is said in the synagogue, when at most the congregants turn to the back of the synagogue (the west) for the last stanza of Lekha Doki, Bo'i Kallah, as is the common custom these days.

However, there are still divergent customs in this matter. Sephardim and some pious Ashkenazim recite Bameh Madlikin *before* Maariv (see *Magen Avraham*, O.H. 204) while most Ashkenazim recite it at the end of Maariv (*BaH* on the Tur, O.H. there). Each custom has its own justification. Those who recite it before Maariv do so because at the end of the chapter [i.e., chap. 2 of Mishnah Shabbat] comes a halakhah which pertains precisely to that time: "A man must say three things in his house before the Sabbath: 'Have you separated the *maaser*? Have you made an *eruv*? Light the candles!'"

On the other hand, those who wait for the end of Maariv have their own reason for doing so. Since Maariv is recited after *pelag ha-minhah*,[13] and it is still daylight when the congregants leave the synagogue, the recitation of Bameh Madlikin was added so that the Sabbath meal would not begin before twilight.[14] Alternatively, *Magen Avraham* suggests that this is to allow time for those who happen to come late to "catch up."

Thus, when the Arizal's custom reached the Ashkenazic community, as in Prague, where the recitation of Bameh Madlikin was at the end of Maariv, there was nothing to separate the two recitations of Mizmor Shir le-Yom ha-Shabbat, and the two were recited one right after the other. Thus was the strange custom of the Altneuschul created. In order to separate the two recitations, however, they added a Kaddish in between. So it seems to me. However, the question of why this oc-

17

curred only in Prague, or even only in the Altneuschul, remains, and awaits a solution.

Before leaving the topic, however, it is worth noting an interesting attempt to explain this custom made by R. Aharon Epstein, who was rabbi in Prague, and which was brought to my attention by R. Dov Goldstein of Alon Shevut. In R. Epstein's work, *Responsa Kappei Aharon* (Munkatch, 5693 [1933]), siman 20, we find the following discussion:

> Regarding [the custom] here in the Altneuschul of reciting Mizmor Shir le-Yom ha-Shabbat twice, with Kaddish in between, it seems to me that, halakhically, the reason is simple. I have seen in *Sefer Tzeror ha-Hayyim* of R. Avraham Emden and in *Sefer Divrei Eleh ha-Brit*[15] and *Sefer Melammed le-Ho'il*[16] that in that holy synagogue they would accompany Lekha Dodi with musical instruments. Thus it is possible that they did so on Erev Shabbat also, and if so, how could this be done, since it is laid down in Shulhan Arukh O.H. 263:4 that our custom is to accept the [prohibitions of the] Sabbath with the recitation of Mizmor Shir le-Yom ha-Shabbat, in the same way as others accept them with the answer to Borkhu. How then could they accompany the mizmor with instrumental music?
>
> This may be the reason they recited the mizmor twice. The first time was merely as the recitation of a mizmor, with instrumental accompaniment, in order to arouse the hearts of the children of Israel to the holiness of Shabbat and the welcoming of the

Sabbath bride, and not as an acceptance of the prohibitions. The second recitation was then for the
purpose of accepting the Sabbath prohibitions, and
was done without musical accompaniment. Later,
even when the musical accompaniment ended, the
custom of a dual recitation remained. So it seems to
me, with God's help.

I have heard that this custom exists in other
synagogues here as well, and it may be that there
too they accompanied the mizmor with music, or
perhaps they merely follow the practice of the
Altneuschul, which has always been the primary
synagogue in Prague to which all others looked for
guidance.

Here we have an explanation for this custom by one
who was a rabbi in Prague. However, the explanation is
built on the assumption, for which there is no evidence
whatsoever, that the mizmor was provided with musical
accompaniment! I therefore prefer the explanation suggested above.

Notes

1. *Minhagei Yisrael*, vol. 4, pp. 1-7. All references are to vol. 1
   unless otherwise noted.
2. See in regard to this S. Hakohen Weingarten, *Nerot Shabbat*
   3 (Adar 5705–II Adar 5706): 175, and the comment of N.
   Ben-Menahem, ibid., p. 186, and that of R. Yosef Golden-
   baum, ibid., pp. 186–187 (my thanks to my dear friend
   Prof. S. Z. Leiman for calling my attention to this source).
   Most recently see A. L. Goldsmith, *The Golem Remembered,
   1904–1980* (Detroit, 1981), pp. 21–50.

As is known, the source of this custom is in the writings of the holy Arizal. See R. Hayyim Sitton's *Eretz ha-Hayyim* (Jerusalem, 5742), O.H. siman 261, pp. 53–54; and *Minhagei ha-Arizal*, Petora de-Abba, p. 33b. And see G. Scholem, *On the Kabbalah and Its Symbolism* (New York, 1965), pp. 202–203.

3. R. Eckstein makes a play on words; *golem* in the Mishnah refers to an uncouth, foolish person.
4. For more of the same, see the article by R. A. Benedikt, "Haggadat Maharal o Aggadat Maharal," *Moriah* 159–160 (Sivan 5745): 102–113, which reveals more forgeries, including the so-called "Haggadah of the Maharal," which never existed.

As for the golem, see most recently M. Idel's *Golem: Jewish Magical and Mystical Traditions on the Artificial Anthropoid* (Albany, N.Y., 1990), pp. 207–231.
5. *Minhagei ha-Ari*, Petora de-Abba (Jerusalem, 5665), 33a–b, according to *Sefer ha-Kavvanot*, Sixth Gate.
6. Which then served as an outer garment.
7. *Shaar ha-Kavvanot* of R. Hayyim Vital, there. Similar testimony is provided by *Hemdat ha-Yamim*, pt. 1, 40d: "Most of the inhabitants of Jerusalem hold to the ancient custom of going outside the city, to the fields, as a body and reciting the Kabbalat Shabbat there."
8. (Venice, 1599) and (Lublin, 1876), 21b.
9. See *Shaar ha-Shammayim*, edited by the Shelah's grandson, R. Avraham Horowitz, which, however, contains many additions that date from after the Shelah. This is clearly based on R. Moshe Cordovero's opinion, cited in *Siddur Tefillah le-Moshe*, Gate 10, siman 4, which is in turn cited in *Tzoluta de-Avraham*, Shabbat, pt. II (Jerusalem, 5751), p. 43. The *Kenesset ha-Gedolah*, O.H. siman 262, reports a similar custom in Constantinople.
10. *Yosef Ometz*, siman 589, p. 125. Lekha Dodi was composed

by R. Shlomo Alkabetz as an acrostic, and the initial letters of the stanzas spell out his name.

11. See most recently R. Y. M. Hillel, *Sefer ha-Ari ve-Gurav* (Jerusalem, 5752), pp. 190–191, for a discussion of these points.
12. See R. Hayyim Sitton, *Eretz ha-Hayyim* (Jerusalem, 5742), p. 54.
13. An hour and a quarter before sunset.
14. See the *BaH*, ad loc.
15. Apparently *Eleh Divrei ha-Brit* (Altona, 5579).
16. The responsa of R. David Tzvi Hoffmann (New York, 5714); see pt. I, siman 16, pp. 14–15.

CHAPTER 2[1]
Mizmor le-Todah During Kabbalat Shabbat

THE HISTORY OF THE CUSTOMS surrounding Kabbalat Shabbat and the recitation of Lekha Dodi has been thoroughly investigated by R. Y. Y. Kohen.[2] He traced the development of this custom through the generations, and demonstrated that it arose in the time of the Sages of Safed in the time of the holy Arizal. At first there were two customs, that of the Arizal and that of R. Moshe Cordovero. According to the first, one was to begin with Mizmor le-David (Psalms 29), a mizmor which contains seven mentions of the word *kol*, "sound," corresponding to the Seven Days of Creation.[3] After that came Lekha Dodi, Mizmor Shir le-Yom ha-Shabbat, and Maariv. However, according to the custom of RaMaK (= R. Moshe Cordovero), they began with Lekhu Nerannenah (Psalms 95), and then continued with another five mizmorim, Psalms 96–99 and 29 (in accordance with the Arizal's custom)—in all, six mizmorim, corresponding to the six days of the work-week.[4] Only after these six mizmorim did they then recite Lekha Dodi and Mizmor Shir le-Yom ha-Shabbat.

Thus, according to the RaMaK's custom, after the six mizmorim corresponding to the days of the work-week, they would receive the Sabbath Queen with the hymn Lekha Dodi, and immediately follow this with Mizmor Shir le-Yom Shabbat as though the Sabbath entered with this seventh mizmor from Psalms. Later on they added the *piyyut* Ana Bekhoah before Lekha Dodi, because its seven verses correspond to the days of the week. Indeed, a few Sephardic siddurim mark each unit of these seven with a separate day of the week.

Thus the structure of the Kabbalat Shabbat service is built on the number seven. And even when additional elements were added they too included this basic numerical symbolism. As an example we may note the common custom in some Sephardic communities to recite yet another seven mizmorim before Lekhu Nerannenah—Psalms 22, 141, 45, 48, 44, 133, 122.[5]

In a modest footnote R. Y. Kohen noted, that some Sephardic communities add an additional mizmor after the five mizmorim of Psalms 95-99—Psalms 100, Mizmor le-Todah.[6] After that they recite Mizmor le-David. It seems to me that this addition has not yet received a satisfactory explanation.

The reason for this would seem to be linked with the

desire of those who established the order of prayer to remain within the structure based on the number seven. Additions to the original seven mizmorim (Mizmor le-Todah, Mizmor le-David, Ana Bekhoah, Perek Bameh Madlikin, and the baraita of Amar R. Eleazar Amar R. Hanina, with Lekha Dodi following) were made, the connection between the first six mizmorim and the seventh (Mizmor Shir le-Yom ha-Shabbat) was broken, to the point that people lost the sense that a sevenfold structure was intended. On the other hand, no one wished to tamper with the order as it was, and so Mizmor le-Todah (Psalms 100) was added as a sixth mizmor after the five taken from Psalms.[7]

In these siddurim the following heading appears before Mizmor le-David: "A mizmor corresponding to the sixth day." From then on this mizmor of "seven sounds" becomes (according to this custom) the seventh mizmor in the order of Kabbalat Shabbat, and not the sixth, as in earlier siddurim.[8]

Notes
1. Hebrew original, vol. 1, pp. 67–70.
2. See his monograph *Seder Qabbalat Shabbat u-Pizmon Lekha Dodi* (Jerusalem, 5729), a preprint from *Sefer Zikaron le-R. Adam-Noah Braun z.l.* (Jerusalem, 5730), pp. 321–357.
3. See Berakhot 29a, Yerushalmi Berakhot 4:7, and the remarks of R. Shraga Abramson in *Leshonenu* 45 (5741): 95.
4. As R. Yaakov Emden explained in his siddur.
5. While I do not understand the reason for the selection of these particular chapters, it should be noted that the last

verse of the last chapter (Psalms 122:9) contains seven words.

6. See *Seder Qabbalat Shabbat*, p. 6, in the note; correct the reference to *Otzar ha-Tefillot*, vol. 1, p. 295b.

7. The addition of Mizmor le-Todah to the Kabbalat Shabbat service was rather innovative, since according to many Rishonim it should not be recited during Shaharit on Shabbat, "since the todah [= the thanksgiving sacrifice] was not offered on the Shabbat" (*Mahzor Vitry*, p. 89). See *Perush ha-Tefillot veha-Berakhot le-R. Yehudah b. Yakar*, Heleq ha-Tefillot, p. 3. So too many other Rishonim, see *Siddur Rashi*, siman 417, p. 208 and siman 494, p. 247; *Orhot Hayyim*, Din Meah Berakhot, siman 20; Tashbetz ha-Qatan, siman 234, among others.

However, the mizmor is cited as part of the Shabbat Shaharit in *Seder Rav Amram Gaon*, pt. II, siman 20 (ed. Goldschmidt, p. 69), and in Provence and Spain it was customary to recite it on Shabbat and Yom Tov, as was the custom in Rome, as is clear from the remarks of R. Zedekiah b. R. Abraham ha-Rofe in *Shibbolei ha-Leqet* 336, siman 76, though it was *not* recited during the workweek! The reason for this is explained by R. Zedekiah in the name of his brother Benjamin as relating to Adam's recitation of Mizmor Shir le-Yom ha-Shabbat as praise and thanksgiving to God for giving him the Sabbath as a day of praise and thanksgiving, and for the future, when, according to the Aggadah (see Leviticus Rabba Tzav 9:7, ed. Margulies, pp. 185–186, "R. Pinhas, R. Levi, R. Yohanan in the name of R. Menahem of Gallia: In the future [= messianic times] all the sacrifices will be abolished except for the todah [= the thanksgiving offering])"—and the Sabbath is an avatar of the messianic age. And so the custom remains in Rome.

The Abudarham justified reciting this mizmor on Shabbat in another way. In responding to *Sefer ha-Manhig*, which forbids saying the mizmor, he writes: "I hold that it is permitted to say it and there is no need to hold back, for the possibility that the Temple will be speedily rebuilt and the thanksgiving offering restored is no reason, since people will not make a mistake [in thinking that, since they recite the mizmor on Shabbat, the offering too should be sacrificed]." The Tur agrees that the mizmor may be recited; see O.H. 281.

Nevertheless, despite all this, the *halakhah le-ma'aseh* for Ashkenazic and Sephardic communities (except for the Roman custom, as noted above) is that Mizmor le-Todah is not recited on Sabbaths or holidays (See *Shiyyurei Knesset ha-Gedolah*, Orah Hayyim, on the Bet Yosef, n. 8; *Ateret Zekenim* and *Kaf ha-Hayyim*, there, n. *nun*). It is therefore somewhat surprising that despite this clear decision regarding Shaharit, it was included in Kabbalat Shabbat. It may be, however, that this is because Kabbalat Shabbat is said just *before* the Shabbat comes in, especially since this is a time at which the thanksgiving offering could still be eaten.

8. In this context it is fitting to note the comment of R. Yehudah b. R. Yakar, in his *Perush ha-Tefillot u-Berakhot* (Jerusalem, 5728), p. 3, regarding the additional mizmorim added to the Shabbat Shaharit prayers. He notes that seven are added in honor of the Sabbath (Ha-Shammayim Mesapperim, Le-David be-Shannoto, Tefillah le-Moshe, Viyhi No'am, She-Omedim be-Veit Ha-Shem, Hodu La-Shem Ki Tov, and Rannenu Tzaddikim), after which another is added, Mizmor Shir le-Yom ha-Shabbat, in order to indicate that the others are indeed in honor of the Sabbath.

CHAPTER 3[1]
Regarding Kiddush

A TYPICAL EXAMPLE of the use of numerology and its consequences can be seen in regard to the wording of the Kiddush for Friday night. According to Seder Rav Amram Gaon (ed. Goldschmidt, vol. 2, p. 66, siman 12), the Rokeah (ed. Shneursohn, siman 52), Mahzor Vitry (p. 144, siman 156), and others, we begin the Kiddush with the word "Va-yekhulu" (Genesis 2:1)—so too Shulhan Arukh, Orah Hayyim 271:10. And that is the wording of the Va-yekhulu which is recited in the Friday night Shemoneh Esreh, which follows the Talmud's teaching that "Whoever recites Va-yekhulu the Torah considers him as Hashem's partner in the Work of Creation" (Shabbat 119b). However, the Rema, the Matteh Moshe (siman 436), and others (including the Arizal)[2] ruled that we should begin with "Yom Ha-Shishi," which is the end of the last verse (Genesis 1:31).

This ruling is surprising, since it goes counter to the Talmudic rule that "we do not divide verses differently than Moshe did" (Berakhot 12b); how then can we lop off two words from the end of a verse? The Matteh Moshe explains:

> Kiddush is made on a full cup of wine by beginning with the words "**Y**om **H**a-Shisi **V**a-Yehkhulu **H**a-Shammayim"—the initial letters of which make up the Tetragrammaton (= the Shem Havayah), while the numerical value of the word "Va-yekhulu" adds up to seventy-two, corresponding to the four-letter Name recombined into the seventy-two-letter [Name]—all symbolizing that the heavens and the earth were created to be God's Throne. Therefore, it is customary to stand at first until the word "Ha-shammayim," which represents the completion of the Name, has been recited.
>
> The *Kolbo* (siman 41) writes that we ought to recite the Kiddush standing, in order to give honor to the King Whom we welcome. However, since Kiddush must be recited where we eat the Shabbat meal, we must sit, for if we stand up and then sit down it appears as a prank.

Thus we learn the three elements which make up the character of the Friday night Kiddush.

(1) The use of the first letters of the first words to make up the Tetragrammaton, despite the halakhic problem involved (see below).

(2) The use of *gematria* to support the appearance of

the Name, together with a kind of midrash to incorporate another word.

(3) The resulting rule that we must stand at the beginning of the Kiddush, even though here too there are halakhic problems.

The matter does not end there, for in the *Sefer Ha-Kavvanot* of R. Hayyim Vital, all of which is based on the Holy Arizal's teachings, we find the following:

> This is the order of the Kiddush. First you say "Yom Ha-Shishi Va-yekhulu Ha-Shammayim," etc., and after that "Savrai Merannan ve-Rabbanan," with the blessing of Bore Peri Ha-Gefen. Then comes the Kiddush proper: ברוך אתה ה׳ אלקינו מלך העולם אשר קדשנו במצותיו ורצה בנו ושבת קדשו באהבה וברצון הנחלתנו זכרון למעשה בראשית תחילה למקראי קודש זכר ליציאת מצרים ושבת קדשך באהבה וברצון הנחלתנו. ברוך אתה ה׳ מקדש השבת. And in the Zohar, Parashat Bereshit (Introduction, 5a), it is explained that there are seventy words in Va-yekhulu and Kiddush itself, thirty-five in each. Therefore, those who are accustomed to add the phrases *"zekher liytziat Mitzrayyim"* and *"ki vanu vaharta ve-otanu kiddashta mi-kol ha-amim ve-Shabbat kodshekha,"* etc., are making a great error, for they are adding to the number of the words. These additions are to be made only during the daytime Kiddush, and those who make this error took the words from there. And the reason for the addition of the two words "Yom Ha-Shishi" before Va-yekhulu is apparently already known, for in this way are the four letters of the Tetragrammaton symbolized.[3]

29

Thus, the employment of the Name of God is here widened to include the entire Kiddush, so that it becomes a combination of words constituting the Divine Name, corresponding to the Seventy-Two-Letter Name, with the addition, of course, of the first two words. And naturally, since the entire Kiddush corresponds to a Divine Name, *the entire Kiddush must be recited while standing*, as the *Shaar Ha-Kavvanot* rules, and not only the first four words.

And so it is recorded in *Peri Etz Hayyim*, chapter 14 of Shabbat: "My master, *zal* [= the Holy Ari] was accustomed to stand for the Kiddush on Shabbat and Yom Tov; afterwards he would seat himself and drink from the Kiddush cup." We see therefore that the exact wording of Kiddush—the Nusah Sepharad version of our time—was established on the basis of number symbolism, and that it overcame another version, that of the Nusah Ashkenaz of our time.

When we examine the Arizal's version carefully, we see that it is made up of two elements: (1) the desire to ensure that Kiddush contains seventy words, and (2) the desire that it contain *seventy-two* words. The first stems from the Zohar, Parashat Vayakhel, 27b, where the Sabbath is described as being adorned with seventy crowns, with the Holy Supernal Name on all sides, which are linked to the verses Vayekhulu ha-shammayim, etc., which contain thirty-five words. "Whoever gives testimony to this and places this [thought] on his heart and will, atones for all his sins."

As far as the second element—the Tetragrammaton, on the one hand, and the Seventy-Two-Letter Name, on the other—is concerned, these were already mentioned by Rabbenu Ephraim, one of the Baalei ha-Tosafot, in his commentary on the Torah:

Va-yekhulu, in *gematria* seventy-two, for the world was created with seventy-two Names, as it is written, "For you said: the world will be built with *hesed* (lovingkindness)" (Psalms 89:3)—and *hesed* in *gematria* is seventy-two. Va-yekhulu **h**a-shammay-im **v**eha-aretz contains the word V-H-V, one Name of the Seventy-Two-Letter Name. The phrase, **Y**om **h**a-shishi, etc., with the yod on one side and the heh on the other, makes up Y-H, together with the other six [letters of the phrase], in order to teach that the Holy One, blessed be He, sealed the six directions with His Name Y-H. **Y**om **h**a-shishi **va**-yekhulu **h**a-shammayim makes up the Tetragram-maton with its initial letters, while the *gematria* of the letters of the Tetragrammaton [with the names of the letters spelled out equals 45, together with the yod-heh [which equals 26, with an additional one added for the "inclusive factor" common in *gematriot*]—yields seventy-two. For all the Explicit Names issue from the Tetragrammaton Y-H-V-H with combinations of the alphabet.[4]

Thus we see that the element of the Seventy-Two-Letter Name is hinted at in various ways in this verse. This motive was transferred to Kiddush by the addition of two words, which not only cause the entire Kiddush to add up to seventy-two words, but themselves symbolize the Tetragrammaton by their initial letters. It is, therefore, perfectly understandable that one should stand while reciting the Kiddush, by whose combinations and permutations we make mention of the Holy and Ineffable Name. However, we stand for another reason, because we give testimony, and when witnesses testify in a Jewish court they do so standing.[5]

It is thus no wonder that the Baalei Tosafot pointed out that the ends of the words "Va-yekhulu," "Bara," "Elokim," and "La'asot" make up the word "Emet," "truth." Both the beginning and the end of Creation are made up of truth, just as at the end of legal documents scribes write "*sharir ve-kayyam*," which verifies the truth of the testimony contained therein.

"We Do Not Divide Verses Differently Than Moshe Did"

The little we have quoted about how the hidden aspects of the Torah influenced the wording of the Friday night Kiddush is sufficient. However, the story does not end there, for, as noted above, the addition of two words to the Kiddush and the recitation of Kiddush while standing involved halakhic problems which have to be dealt with. R. Mordekhai Yaffeh, the author of the *Levushim*, recommended that one begin the Kiddush in a low tone with the words "*va-yehi erev ve-yehi voker*," and then recite the rest in a louder voice, so as to distinguish the additions from the rest (*Levush ha-Hur*, O.H. 271:10). This addition of still another four words to the Kiddush (albeit in a low tone) was certainly intended to keep the two words "*yom ha-shishi*" from being recited alone, as an isolated part of the verse. With the *Levush*'s addition, the one who says Kiddush will recite a "complete" half-verse at the start.

The Hatam Sofer discusses this custom in his responsa (O.H. 10).

Some cast doubt on the custom of beginning Friday night Kiddush with "*va-yehi erev ve-yehi voker*," which begins in the middle of a verse. In order to reconcile this custom with the Halakhah I will suggest the following. The words "*yom ha-shishi*" are the essential addition to the Kiddush; they are added in order to symbolize the Tetragrammaton with the initial letters of "*yom ha-shishi va-yekhulu ha-shammayim*," but it is not proper to begin with "*yom ha-shishi*," which has no real meaning—"the sixth day and the heavens were finished." Therefore, the words "*va-yehi erev ve-yehi voker*" were added, in order to give the two essential words a context of their own. What would you have? That we add the first half of the verse as well? "The Lord saw all that He had done, and behold, it was very good"? It is not proper to do so on the Sabbath eve, because of the midrash that equates "very good" (מאד) with death (מות).[6] And so, since it is not possible to add a context to the two words "*yom ha-shishi*" in any other way, it is permitted to divide the verse in a way which does not have Sinaitic warrant. So it seems to me in order to justify this custom.

Moreover, there is another reason to permit it, for the Hatam Sofer solved the problem on the basis of a comment in *Magen Gibborim* by R. Mordekhai Zev Ettinga and R. Yosef Shaul Nathansohn (Lvov, 5592, Zolkiew, 5599), the "two brothers-in-law" to whom the question was directed, and who wrote that where the verse is punctuated with an *etnahta* or a *zakef katan*, it is permitted, and such a division is not considered as one which Moshe did not make. And, of course, there is an *etnahta* before *"va-yehi erev ve-yehi voker."*

The author of *Torah Shelemah*, R. Menahem Mendel Kasher, has suggested another explanation, based on a statement in the Yerushalmi Megilla 4:2, which classifies *"va-yehi erev ve-yehi voker"* as a separate verse when necessary, such as when two *aliyot* must be fit within the five verses of that parashah.[7] Ordinarily, each would be given a minimum of three verses, but since only five are available, the Talmud suggests dividing the five verses into two parts, since the words *"va-yehi erev ve-yehi voker"* do appear elsewhere as a separate verse (Genesis 1:13, 19, 23).[8] Therefore, even though this clause appears as part of a longer verse here, we nevertheless may separate it when necessary, as in Friday night Kiddush.

However, Reuven Margaliot, in his *Nefesh Hayyah*,[9] suggests yet another explanation.

It would seem that if one begins a verse he must complete it and not stop in the middle, but it is permitted to *begin* in the middle of a verse. This rule would explain why we begin with *"yom ha-shishi va-yekhulu ha-shammayim."* Thus too we understand why we are permitted to begin in the middle of a verse when we make Kiddush on Shabbat morning, when we say: על כן ברך ה׳ את יום השבת ויקדשהו (Exodus 20:11), which constitutes the second half of the verse of the Ten Commandments in respect to Shabbat.

This question was already directed to the Hatam Sofer . . . and the Maharam Schick (Orah Hayyim 124); it is clear that the Torah was concerned that we not end in the middle of a verse which we have begun, but we are permitted to *begin* a verse in the middle, as we learn in the mishnah of Bikkurim 3:6: While [the basket] is still on his shoulder he reads "I have recited before God today" to the end [= the "confession" recited when bringing the First Fruits to the Temple, see Deuteronomy 26:11]. Note that the recitation begins in the middle of a verse. Another proof may be cited from the Talmud—Berakhot 28b: R. Eliezer says: Whoever travels in a place of danger may pray a short Shemoneh Esreh and say: "Save, O God, your nation, the remnant of Israel"—even though this is the second half of a verse in Jeremiah 31:6.

However it may be, it is clear that the addition of the two words "*yom ha-shishi*" led to another addition in its wake, the words "*va-yehi erev ve-yehi voker.*" However, since these words did not aid the "creation" of the Tetragrammaton, and indeed impeded the Seventy-Two-Letter Name from being represented, it was suggested that they should be recited in a low voice. This constitutes a compromise between recitation and non-recitation.[9]*

Even when the addition was permitted, however, it was limited by the qualification that "one should pause a little between 'yom ha-shishi' and 'va-yekhulu ha-shammayim' in order to indicate that they are not one verse."[10] Another such compromise has been suggested, as we find in Siddur Bet Yaakov, which is based on R. Yaakov Emden's Shaar ha-Shammayim, p. 152, where we are advised to recite the first half of the verse in a low tone, "The Lord saw all that he had done, and behold, it was very good," וירא אלקים את כל אשר עשה ויהי טוב מאד ויהי ערב ויהי בקר וכו׳. It appears that the intention is to say the whole verse, including "va-yehi erev va-yehi voker," in a low tone, and in this way the problem of dividing the verse in a manner not sanctioned at Mattan Torah was solved.

Kiddush Standing Or Sitting?

There remains the question of whether one sits or stands for Kiddush before the meal. The Rema (O.H. 271:1) writes: "One may stand while saying Kiddush, but it is better to sit (Kolbo), and it is the custom to sit even when one recites Va-yekhulu. But when one begins [the Kiddush] one stands a bit for God's honor."[11] His decision is close to that of the Levush, part of whose opinion we cited above.[12]

In contrast, a number of Poskim preferred the custom of standing during Kiddush, since its recitation[13] is similar to testifying [to God's creation of the world, and testimony must be given standing].[14] So too is the opinion expressed in the *Sefer Pardes* of Rashi.

> Because of the [people's] devotion to giving [this] testimony, they do so once again at their tables and recite Va-yekhulu before saying the Kiddush. People have become accustomed to doing so while sitting because most of them are [reciting Kiddush] individually in their own homes, and therefore formal testimony, which requires two or three witnesses, cannot be given. And so, in order that it not appear that we are following two [separate] Torahs—with some people giving testimony, and some not—everyone stands, even though each is an individual.[15]

This opinion and this custom were not accepted by all Rishonim. For example, we find that R. Zedekiah b. R. Benjamin the Physician, the author of *Shibbolei ha-Leqet*, wrote in siman 66 that his brother Benjamin had written the following:

> The custom of saying [Va-yekhulu] standing has arisen because people are still standing after having recited the silent Amidah, and will have to stand again for the repetition of it afterwards as one blessing which symbolizes the seven [of the Friday night Maariv Amidah; people therefore remain standing for Va-yekhulu,] not for reasons of testimony,[16] and whoever says it while sitting has not lost [anything

thereby]. A proof of this is that people sit while reciting Kiddush the next morning. Nevertheless, one should not change ancient customs.

However, we have already seen that the Rema cites the *Kolbo* to the effect that it is better to sit. And the Mishnah Berurah explains that this better fulfills the requirement of "Kiddush at the place of the meal," since one sits where one will eat.[17]

The GRA was even more insistent on sitting during Kiddush. In his comments to Orah Hayyim 271, s.v. *ve-yoter tov*, he notes that Tosafot's statement (Berakhot 43a, s.v. *ho'il*) reflects the essential halakha. Tosafot write:

We must examine our custom of standing during Havdallah, since how can we fulfill the requirement for each other, since we are not sitting or reclining? Perhaps this is because we set ourselves to fulfill the requirement of Havdallah, and so this mind-set serves for everything. It is therefore proper for the one reciting the Havdallah and those who are listening to sit, so that it will appear as though we are set [for the mitzvah], and the [one reciting] fulfills the requirement for the others.

The same rule applies to Kiddush, and so, according to the GRA, one should sit during Kiddush. Furthermore, an additional reason has been suggested for not allowing standing, at least during the drinking of the wine; it is not proper for a *talmid hakham* to eat and drink

while standing,[18] as the Matteh Moshe wrote in siman
509 in regard to Havdallah. It is for this reason that even
those who stand for Kiddush sit to drink the wine.[19]

The Compromise Regarding Kiddush

From the foregoing it is clear that Kiddusha Rabba, i.e.,
Shabbat morning Kiddush, should be said while sitting,
since, apparently, there are no symbolic Names and kabbalistic secrets enshrined therein, nor testimony regarding Creation—in short, no special reason to stand.
And indeed, most of those who stand for Friday night
Kiddush sit for the morning Kiddush. However, there
are those who stand then too, either because of the habit
of standing for Kiddush on Friday night or because of
hidden reasons regarding the greater holiness associated
with standing for Kabbalistic reasons.[20] Accordingly,
they transferred the custom of standing on Friday night
to Shabbat morning as well.

This range of customs has spread far and wide, even
to far-off Yemen, as R. Yosef Kafih writes in his well-
known work, *Halikhot Teiman*: "Some are accustomed to
make Kiddush standing, some say Va-yekhulu standing,
some say the entire Kiddush sitting. Where they recite
the Kiddush standing, it is the custom for only the men
to stand, for Va-yekhulu is equivalent to testimony, and
women cannot testify."[21] In Morocco, too, it is the custom for women not to stand.

Notes

1. From vol. 2, pp. 158–171.
2. See *Minhagei Ha-Ari Petora de-Abba* (Jerusalem, 5665; reprinted., Jerusalem, 5745), siman 21, p. 34b.
3. Sixth Gate, "Shaar Ha-Kavvanot" (Jerusalem, 5723), p. 71b.
4. *Perush ha-Torah le-Baalei ha-Tosafot*, ed. Gellis, vol. 1 (Jerusalem, 5742), p. 75, n. 5.
5. This point was already made by the *Daat Zekenim mi-Baalei ha-Tosafot, Perush ha-Torah le-Baalei Tosafot*, ed. Gellis, p. 77, n. 7.
6. See Genesis Rabba 9:10.
7. See *Torah Shelemah*, vol. 1 (Jerusalem, 5697), siman 418.
8. See also Rashi on Taanit 27b.
9. (Tel Aviv, 5714), Milluim, pp. 3–4.
9*. On this issue, see *Minhagei Yisrael* vol. 4 (1995), pp. 23–28).
10. *Cited in Otzar ha-Tefillot*, p. 645.
11. So too in the "Rav's Shulhan Arukh," siman 271, where he notes that "the custom has spread of sitting during the recitation of Va-yekhulu . . . since it was already said standing during the synagogue service. . . . Nevertheless people stand a bit when they begin 'Yom Ha-Shishi' . . . since the initial letters hint at the Tetragrammaton." See Hillel Halevi, *Kiddush Ke-Hilkhato* (Bnei Brak, 1989), p. 108.
12. Above, p. 32.
13. Or rather, the recitation of Va-yekhulu; see Shabbat 119b.
14. Shevuot 30a.
15. Ed. Ehrenreich, p. 310. See also *Kiddush Ke-Hilkhato*, pp. 107–108.

My dear son David pointed out to me the opinion of the Hazon Ish to Orah Hayyim 37:10 (p. 114): "It is possible that there is no need . . . [to recite Kiddush] standing, for we do not find any Poskim suggesting such an innovation. . . . [Furthermore,] there is no need to exert oneself [to find another person as a second] witness, for we do not find any Poskim suggesting this. [Likewise,] we ought to be concerned over the appearance of setting up witnesses for the Creation, inasmuch as the TaZ wrote that an individual should not recite Va-yekhulu, for such testimony is not relevant to individuals. [But] this point is debatable, since individuals certainly recite Va-yekhulu during [the silent] Amidah . . . and what of it, since the essential thing is the mitzvah, faith, and the acceptance of the Sabbath laws."

16. I. Ta-Shema, in an article in *Asufot* 1 (5747): 339, cites a comment found in the margin of *Halakhot Gedolot*, ed. Hildesheimer (Jerusalem, 5732), p. 507, in which it is written: "People should stand in the synagogue until the *sheliah tzibbur* recites Kiddush over a cup of wine, until the very end, and not sit, because [standing] is good for the knees." Ta-Shema discusses the date of this comment, and proves that it is very early, that R. Y. Bargeloni had it before him, and it may perhaps stem from *Seder Rav Amram Gaon*. That is, just as the Rishonim state that the Friday night Kiddush is healthy for the eyes (see Ta-Shema there), so too is standing good for strengthening the knees. In any case, however, it is clear that anyone who does not wish to strengthen his knees is free to sit during Kiddush.

17. We will not go into the question of the sources of the requirement, whether it is of biblical origin or *mide-Rabbanan*, if it is permitted to make Kiddush in one place and eat in another. As to the last, see the *Likkutei Maharih* of R. Israel Hayyim Friedmann (5660; reprint ed., Jerusalem, 5725), II, 31a–b, and in the above-mentioned article by Ta-Shema in *Asufot*.

18. See Gittin 70a, Derekh Eretz Zuta 5:1, and the revised version of my edition of Derekh Eretz Zuta (Jerusalem, 5742), p. 124, where I indicated a number of Rishonim who quote this statement. See also *Kaf ha-Hayyim* 271, n. 64, and

Siddur ha-Arizal (= *Seder ha-Tefillah*, Zolkiew, 5541), p. 115b: "And after that [= Kiddush] he sits and drinks, with his back to the north while facing the candles."

19. We will not go into the matter of sitting or standing during Havdallah; see *Encyclopedia Talmudit*, vol. 8, p. 81. On a related matter, R. Yaakov Hayyim Zemah suggests in his *Nagid u-Metzavveh* (reprint ed., n.d.), p. 53, that one must give charity to a poor man while standing, for the Shekhinah sits on the ground, and the giver must raise Her up by means of the charity he gives. Compare R. Yosef Yaavetz's statement, in his commentary to Avot 1:5, that the Shekhinah rests between the shoulders of the poor, and welcoming the poor is a great and exalted mitzvah. See also the comments of my father and teacher, HaRav Shmuel Sperber, in his work *Maamarot* (Jerusalem, 5738), p. 190.

20. As set down in *Siddur ha-Arizal* (Zolkiew, 5541), p. 128b. On the other hand, see *Sefer Vayaged Moshe* of R. Moshe Yehudah Katz (Brooklyn, 5740), pp. 88–89, that even those who stand for Kiddush on Shabbat sit for Kiddush during the Passover seder.

21. R. Y. Kafih, *Halikhot Teiman* (Jerusalem, 5728), p. 5, note *.

CHAPTER 4[1]
Kiddush During Seudah Shelishit

DR. YAAKOV GARTNER, in his article "Seudah Shelishit—
Hebetim Hilkatiyyim ve-Historiyyim,"[2] parts 1 and 2,
described two customs which slowly crystallized over
the generations; in one case Seudah Shelishit came in the
afternoon, after Minhah, while according to the second,
somewhat surprising, custom, the morning meal was
divided into two parts, one called Seudah Sheniyah, and
the other, Seudah Shelishit.

It would seem that several other different customs
regarding Seudah Shelishit may be explained against this
background. The custom of reciting Kiddush before this
meal is known from several Ashkenazic, Sephardic, and
Oriental communities. The wording is as follows:
ויאמר משה אכלוהו היום כי שבת היום לה׳ ... על כן ברך ה׳ את יום השבת
ויקדשהו. בא׳׳י בורא פרי הגפן. However, the more common custom is to limit Kiddush to the first two Sabbath meals.

Some attribute this custom to the Rambam in Hilkhot Shabbat 30:9: "Each of the three Sabbath meals
must be accompanied (*likvo'a*) by wine and the breaking
of the bread of two hallot."[3]

The Meiri understood the Rambam in this way: "So
wrote the great codifier [the Rambam] that even this
Kiddush [Kiddusha Rabba in the morning] must be recited where the meal will be eaten, and so too *at every
meal during the day*."[4] (This implies that the Rambam is
referring to more than one daytime meal.) So too the
author of *Sefer ha-Mikhtam* (Pesahim, p. 90): "Again, the
Rambam wrote that even the meal at Minhah time must
be accompanied by wine." So too the author of *Sefer
ha-Minhagot*, R. Asher b. R. Saul of Lunel: "He [the Ram-
bam] perhaps referred to Kiddusha Rabba as necessary
[i.e., at Seudah Shelishit]."[5] And so Rabbenu Yonah understood the Rambam, though he disagreed with him.[6]
This matter was cited in the Tur, Orah Hayyim 291: "The
Rambam wrote that one should set Seudah Shelishit on
wine . . . but my master, my father the Rosh, z.l., did not
make a blessing on the wine first."

However, the Bet Yosef writes there that:

Rabbenu Yonah[7] . . . wrote in the name of the
Ramah [R. Meir ha-Levi Abulafia] that there is no
need to say Kiddush at Seudah Shelishit, and so too
wrote the *Mordekhai*[8] . . . and the Responsa of the
Ramban, siman 214. . . .[9] In truth, the words of the
Rambam are not all that clear that one must recite
Kiddush over wine at Seudah Shelishit, for it is

possible to interpret them as referring merely to *drinking wine during the meal,* and since all [!] the Poskim explain that one need not make Kiddush, and also, since the Rambam's language is not clear, we do not do so. Nevertheless, one who does so has not lost [anything thereby].

Support for this position comes from the *Haggahot Bet Yosef* there: "After that I saw that the Rambam wrote [elsewhere] in 29[:10] [in Hilkhot Shabbat], 'It is a mitzvah to make a blessing over wine on the Sabbath before one eats one's second meal, and this is called Kiddusha Rabba.'"[10] This implies that there is no mitzvah to do so for Seudah Shelishit.

However, it is clear that the custom of Kiddush for Seudah Shelishit was not created by a misunderstanding of the words of the Rambam, for we find it in several sources even before the Rambam, and also where they are not dependent on him. Thus, for example, in the Geonic responsum quoted in *Mahzor Vitry,* siman 135 (p. 107): "And so there are those who make Kiddush over wine for the third [meal], for the word 'today' [which appears three times in Exodus 16:25] refers to three meals, and why should one meal be given preference over another?" The Ravyah also refers to this custom, though he does not endorse it (siman 252, vol. 1, p. 335), and so too perhaps is another Geonic decision cited in *Sefer ha-Itim* of R. Y. Bargeloni, siman 195 (p. 284 = *Shaarei Teshuvah* 140).

This custom is known from Italy, as we learn from

the *Shibbolei ha-Leqet,* siman 93 (ed. Mirsky, p. 328), though no reason is given.

It seems to me that the reason for the development of this division of customs, i.e., whether to make Kiddush for Seudah Shelishit or not, depends on the division regarding the time for this meal. As long as it is eaten after midday, and certainly after Minhah, as is the custom in most communities, and is thus a separate and independent meal, it would be accompanied by a Kiddush of its own. However, where it is merely the second half of the second meal, the Kiddusha Rabba for that meal would serve for this one as well, since another Kiddush might well be thought of as a *berakhah le-vattalah,* a vain blessing, or at least a blessing for which there is no need (*berakhah she-eina tzerikha*). This was the opinion of the *Or Zarua* (Hilkhot Shabbat, siman 52, 23a): "Moreover, it seems to me that wherever one may fulfill his obligation with one blessing but brings about a situation where he requires a second, this second one is a vain blessing (*berakhah le-vattalah*)." This too is the opinion of the Ri in Tosafot Shabbat 118a, s.v. *be-minhah.*

However, an almost polemical tone of rationalization is felt in the words of even those who tended to a positive opinion regarding the saying of Kiddush for the divided second meal. So, for example, in the words of the *Or Zarua:*

Not only is it necessary to say the Birkat ha-Mazon [after the first half-meal], and it is forbidden to taste anything until they do so, but even if one said,

"Let us bless [Birkat ha-Mazon]" or "Wash, and let us bless Birkat ha-Mazon," it is forbidden to taste anything until they do so. Therefore they must make a Hamotzi and a blessing over the wine [before beginning the second half-meal]. If this was not done, it is forbidden to eat and drink. And this is the accepted Halakhah in Israel.

Similarly, a Geonic responsum in the *Or Zarua* there (= *Otzar ha-Geonim*, Shabbat, responsum 106, siman 326):

And that which you asked regarding Hamotzi and the blessing on the wine for the second [= third] meal, which comes first? We saw regarding the first meal [of the day] that we must certainly make the blessing over the wine first, for R. Yehudah[11] said: bringing a cup of wine and making the blessing over the wine and drinking for the honor of the Sabbath, then washing the hands, blessing Hamotzi and finishing the meal, blessing Birkat ha-mazon and making a blessing over the wine [for Seudah Shelishit]; they drink and then wash their hands again, making the blessing for hand-washing; they make the Hamotzi and then eat again [the third meal, according to R. B. M. Lewin there]. If they want to drink they make the blessing over wine again and drink, for since they have already recited the Birkat ha-Mazon for the first meal, they are forbidden to eat and drink until they recite Hamotzi and the blessing over the wine.

47

Note the need to emphasize and reemphasize the requirement of Kiddush and hand-washing a second time after the first Birkat ha-Mazon. It should be understood without comment that they must wash and make a Motzi' if they wish to eat again after Birkat ha-Mazon, even though what we really are talking about is one long meal. However, were these not felt to be unnecessary blessings? Moreover, there were those who did not even require Birkat ha-Mazon between the two half-meals, as in Italy, according to *Shibbolei ha-Leqet*. And according to them, it was all the more certain that Kiddush was an unnecessary blessing.

Those who held to this ancient custom felt the need to justify it with additional considerations, even though the additional Kiddush was due to the fact that the meals were now eaten one after the other. Thus, we find the Rosh writing in his responsa (Kelal 22, siman 4), that since they do this for the honor of the Sabbath, in order to fulfill the mitzvah of eating a third meal, the Kiddush is not considered an unnecessary blessing; compare the Tosafot noted above.

Those who did away with this custom clearly did so because of the consideration of an unnecessary blessing. The custom of not reciting a third Kiddush spread even to communities where the third meal was spaced well after the second; they needed a reason for *not* making a third Kiddush. Thus, the *Shibbolei ha-Leqet* writes that Kiddush should not be said because most of the Sabbath had already passed, and Kiddush had already been recited for the second meal in the morning (siman 93, ed. Mirsky, p. 328)—implying that the Seudah Shelishit was eaten in the afternoon.

In summary, it appears that the custom of dividing the second meal into two parts caused the weakening of the saying of Kiddush for Seudah Shelishit. Just as the first custom gradually disappeared, so too did the second, in most communities. However, there were still those who required the drinking of wine during the meal, according to the opinion of the Rambam,[12] to make sure that the meal was accompanied by wine. This requirement was perhaps an echo of the ancient custom of Kiddush at Seudah Shelishit.

Notes
1. From vol. 1, pp. 82–87.
2. *Sidra* 5 (5749); and see Y. Weinstock, *Be-Maagalei ha-Niglah veha-Nistar* (Jerusalem, 5730), pp. 281–282, and now in his *Gilgulei Minhag be-Olam ha-Halakhah* (Jerusalem, 1995), pp. 171–191.
3. See the illuminating remarks of R. Gedaliah Felder, *Siddur Yeshodei Yeshurun* (Jerusalem, 5741), pp. 513–514.
4. See the Meiri to Pesahim 106a, p. 226.
5. S. Asaf, *Sifran shel Rishonim* (Jerusalem, 5695), p. 181.
6. See Rabbenu Yonah to the Rif, Berakhot, chap. 3, p. 36b in the numbering for the Rif).
7. As noted above.
8. Shabbat, siman 397, and see there a comment in the name of the Rosh.
9. See the Responsa of the Rashba attributed to the Ramban, siman 210: "Therefore my master R. Moshe [the Ramban?], z.l., said that it is good to squeeze apples or pears and

knead them with their juices, and so too was he accustomed to make a Motzi on two hallot for Seudah Shelishit. But he would not make a blessing over wine beforehand."

10. These comments are from the Bet Yosef himself, but were originally called *Bedek ha-Bayit* when they were first published in Salonica in 5365, Venice 5366, Cracow 5370 (?); they then entered editions of the Tur. See *Sarei ha-Elef*, 2nd ed. (Jerusalem, 5739), p. 367, n. 23. It appears that this is the opinion of the *Peri Etz ha-Hayyim* (Shaar 18, par. 18), and so the Yaavetz (= R. Yaakov Emden) decided in his siddur—and this against the opinion of the Shelah, who cited the Arizal. See *Yesodei Yeshurun* there, p. 514.

11. Either R. Sherira Gaon's grandfather or R. Yehudai Gaon, according to the note of R. B. M. Lewin in *Otzar ha-Geonim*.

12. The *BaH* in the name of Maharam Alashkar, the Magen Avraham in the name of the *Tikkunei Shabbat*, and *Siddur ha-Shelah* give a reason for this: Moses, Joseph, and David all passed away at Minhah time, as explained in the Holy Zohar, and so drinking wine is considered a consolation. See also *Likkutei Maharih* (R. Yisrael Hayyim Friedmann, 5760), vol. 2, p. 76b.

PART II
PASSOVER

CHAPTER 5[1]
Shemurah Matzah from the Time of Reaping[2]

THERE ARE THREE DEGREES OF STRINGENCY mentioned in connection with shemurah matzah, as expressed by R. Yosef Karo in Shulhan Arukh.

It is proper (*tov*) to keep[3] (*lishmor*) the wheat from which the matzah used for the mitzvah of eating matzah is made, so that no water falls on it from the time of reaping, or at least from the time of grinding, and in times of scarcity (*she'at ha-dehak*)[4] it is permitted to buy [flour][5] from the market.[6]

The meaning of "it is permitted to buy from the market" is that it is possible to buy flour which has not been kept from water ("unguarded flour") from the market, and so the "guarding" begins from the time of kneading. Thus there are three degrees: (1) from the time of reaping, the most desirable category; (2) from the time of grinding; (3) from the time of kneading, which is permitted only in times of scarcity.

It has been noted that the third category, which R. Yosef Karo terms *"she'at ha-dehak,"* was actually the most commonly observed in the time of the Tannaim, Amoraim, and Geonim.[7] The second degree, which R. Karo introduces with the phrase "at least," is the custom of Rashi's school, i.e., the custom of France and even Germany.[8] This approach is explained in the Rosh to Pesahim, "The custom in Germany and France is to keep it from water from the time of grinding, for *it is then that it is brought close to water, for it is ground in water-powered mills.*[9]

The Magen Avraham notes in this connection that in places where the mill is powered by animals or wind, there is no need for guarding [at that point].[10]

As to the category which R. Karo recommends as the most desirable, and which has become an essential part of the mitzvah of matzah in our time, it is precisely this which has no explicit source in the Talmud.

There are two elements to R. Karo's formulation: It is proper to guard it (1) so that no water fall on it, (2) from the time of reaping. Each of these has a source of its own. The first comes from the She'iltot: "One does not fulfill the mitzvah of eating matzah except with matzah which has been kept from leavening for the sake of matzah *from when water falls on it*,"[11] though from the language it is impossible to conclude with any assurance that this refers to guarding from the time of reaping. It may well be that this refers to guarding from the time of kneading, when "water" certainly "falls on it,"[12] or from the time of grinding, when water wheels are used, as noted above, or, perhaps, in a case when the wheat is transported by boat, when there is a serious possibility that the wheat would be moistened.[13] In conclusion, therefore, the She'iltot here teaches us only that we must be careful when water is involved.

The second element in the formulation of R. Karo, the words "from the time of reaping," is first mentioned in the Rif to Pesahim 40a: "People should guard their Passover flour from the time of reaping, as it is written, 'And guard the matzot' (Exodus 12:17), and Rava said to those who were binding sheaves: 'When you handle [them], handle [them keeping in mind that it is] for the purpose of [the mitzvah of eating] matzah [on Passover], i.e., take care that no water fall on it.' The meaning of *kefei* is 'sheaves.'" Thus, the Rif learned the rule of *matzah mi-she'at ketzirah* from Rava's statement in Pesahim there: "When you handle [them], handle [them keeping in mind that it is] for the purpose of [the mitzvah of eating] matzah [on Passover]," or: "for the purpose of the mitzvah [of eating matzah on Passover]."[14]

The Rif's opinion on this matter was accepted by the

Sages of Provence and Spain. *Sefer Orah* combined the two elements—the opinion of the She'iltot and that of the Rif—and laid down the following rule:

> People should guard this wheat so that water does not fall on it while it is still rooted, or dew during the night, and one must guard this wheat from the time of reaping on, laying it out in a closed storehouse in a hidden place in order that neither water nor dew fall on it, and that is the [proper] way of guarding it, as the verse says: "And guard the matzot" (Exodus 12:17); and *shimmur me-ikara* [guarding from the start][15] is required, as Rava said to those who were binding sheaves: "When you handle [them], handle [them keeping in mind that it is] for the purpose of [the mitzvah of eating] matzah [on Passover]."[16]

However, Rabbenu Yeruham combined them entirely, as though both elements came from the She'iltot: "And in She'iltot it is written: 'One does not fulfill the obligation of matzah except with [matzah] which was kept from leavening from the time that water may have fallen on it from reaping.'"[17] So too the Tur in the name of the Rif: "Rav Alfas wrote that guarding the wheat from which we fulfill our requirement of matzah [on Passover] is from the time of reaping so that no water falls on it."[18]

However, even if we accept the interpretation of the Rif and those who follow him, that the word *kefei* means "sheaves" in Pesahim 40a, the matter is still difficult, since handling sheaves is still a stage in the process of preparing matzah which comes *after* reaping, and therefore the obligation of guarding begins only at the time of handling the sheaves. Even more difficult are Rava's instructions to those binding the sheaves to do so with the mitzvah in mind; why did he not simply instruct them to do so from the time of reaping?

Here I would suggest that the word hitherto translated as "handling," *hafakh*, should rather be translated by "turn around to all sides." The process involved is the usual way of *drying* sheaves which had become wet—to turn them from side to side until all sides had dried in the sunlight.[19] In this connection one may refer to the description of Columella, a Roman author of the first half of the first century, who wrote a guide to agriculture (*Res Rustica*), wherein he describes how to dry grain which had become wet in a sudden rain. He explains that "if all of it is wet, there is no reason to turn it about when it is still dripping; rather, it is better to place the upper part in the sun to dry, and only after that to turn it over (*tunc demun convertemus*), and only when [the grain] is dry on both sides" are the sheaves bound.[20]

Rava's instructions, then, were perhaps given in special circumstances—when the sheaves had become wet and it was necessary to dry them by turning them from side to side in the sun. He instructed those who were doing so to have in mind that they were doing so for the sake of the mitzvah. If this suggestion is correct, then Rava's instructions have nothing to do with guarding ordinary wheat from the time of reaping; they referred only to grain which had become wet—"on which water had fallen," as the She'iltot put it. The Rif's explanation certainly came to him by tradition, but it is not absolutely required by the sugya, and the Talmud's words can be explained in a different way.

Of the three views cited in the Shulhan Arukh, the last one, the one recommended only in times of scarcity or other problems, is the basic one—the one which was the most common from the time of the Tannaim to that of the Geonim. The one introduced by the phrase "at least" is identified with Germany and France, and depended on the special conditions of that time and place—the use of water-powered mills, where moistening the grain during the grinding process was a real danger.

But the view which is most highly recommended by R. Yosef Karo, who describes it as "proper," has no explicit source in the Talmud, and seems to be based on the Rif's explanation of Rava's instructions—instructions which may be explained otherwise. The Rif's interpretation was combined with that of the She'iltot, which apparently was intended for conditions which had nothing to do with guarding from the time of reaping, a phrase which is not mentioned at all in the She'iltot. It is precisely this view, which has the least support in the sources, that has spread and been accepted within most Jewish communities as the customary one—"Shemurah Matzah."[21]

Hasidim and Matzah Guarded from the Time of Reaping
The concern to keep wheat kernels from coming into

contact with water—which "prepares" them to become ritually impure—is mentioned in connection with those who wished to eat ordinary food (i.e., not from sacrifices or from priestly or levitical gifts, such as *terumah* or *maaser*) in a state of ritual purity (*toharah*). Interestingly enough, this has become a matter of concern in the last two centuries, but in a context totally different from the original one.

We mentioned above that the view that had the weakest support in the sources in regard to guarding wheat intended for matzah on Passover—from the time of reaping—was the one which became "normative" among Ashkenazim, as the custom of the *"mehadrin min ha-mehadrin,"* though at first it was only the custom of men who were especially pious and were known as such; as the Maharil put it, *"hasidim ve-anshei ma'aseh."*[22] He himself noted that others, himself included, were not so careful and watched the wheat only from the time of grinding.

Even R. Yehezkel Landau, the "Noda Bi-Yehudah," who lived in Prague about three centuries after the Maharil,[23] responds to one inquirer that only the *mehadrin min ha-mehadrin* in all the districts of Poland observe this stringency; no one else pays attention to it (*let de-hash leh*).[24] And even though the Vilna Gaon was very strict in this matter,[25] his disciples did not follow him in this.[26]

What the Vilna Gaon's disciples did not do, however, was done by those whom he opposed with all his might. This stringent custom, keeping grain from contact with moisture from the time of reaping, spread in Poland, Ukraine, and Galicia among all the Hasidim of Chernobyl, Ruzhin, Lublin, and Kotzk. And most of them were careful in this matter for the first seven days of Passover, just as the Vilna Gaon had been![27]

In general, Hasidic laws and customs were not written down, but spread by word of mouth; it was sufficient for word of the rebbe's customs to be passed along to his followers for them to adopt the customs as their own.[28] In this respect Hasidism had greater power over its adherents than movements opposed to it had over theirs, and it was this which caused the spread of the custom of *mehadrin* in regard to keeping matzah from contact with water from the time of reaping.

The Blessing *Al Akhilat Matzah*

In this connection I will mention yet another custom regarding which Hasidim seem to have adopted the Vilna Gaon's custom—this too in regard to the Passover laws. It is well known that there are differences among the Rishonim as to whether the eating of matzah after the first day of Passover is a mitzvah or not. Some, like the Baal HaMaor, hold that it is,[29] but others, including the Shulhan Arukh, decided that there is no obligation except on the first night.[30] The Vilna Gaon held that it was a mitzvah to eat matzah each day of Passover. "All seven [days it is a] mitzvah, and it is called 'voluntary' (*reshut*) only in comparison with the first night's obligation, and a ['mere'] mitzvah is considered 'voluntary' in comparison with an obligation. Despite this appellation of *reshut* it is a Torah mitzvah. . . . He [= the Vilna Gaon] treasured this mitzvah of eating matzah all the days of Passover."[31]

Now, the question arises of whether to recite the blessing "*al akhilat matzah*" on eating matzah throughout Passover. Some Aharonim hold that this is not considered a vain *berakhah*; among them are the Netziv[32] and the *Yafeh Le-lev*.[33] On the other side are the Maharsham,[34] the Hatam Sofer,[35] in accordance with the ruling of the Magen Avraham at the end of O.H. 639, and also the Vilna Gaon.[36]

The *Sedei Hemed* cites the following:

I became aware that in this city there were many householders (*baalei batim*) and some others who were more familiar with Jewish law (*mevinim*) who were accustomed to recite the blessing "*al akhilat matzah*" each day of Passover—day and night. . . . I trembled at the thought of it; on investigation it proved to be true. I announced through all the synagogues in town that they should not make this vain *berakhah* (*berakhah le-vattalah*), for this custom has no basis, in my opinion, and is a mistake.[37]

We discover the identity of these people in the Maharsham's responsum:

Regarding the custom of this sect of Hasidim who follow someone known as a "tzaddik" to recite the

blessing *"al akhilat matzah"* all through Passover. . . .
It is not proper to do so, and so the spirit of the
Sages is distressed with these Hasidim and their
leader. Aside from the prohibition of reciting a vain
berakhah, there is the matter of interrupting the con-
tinuity of the Motzi' and the eating of the bread
(*"hefsek"*). The result is that [despite having recited
two *berakhot*] they have in effect eaten bread without any effective blessing. This custom should be
stopped.[38]

Thus we see that there were Hasidim who seem to have
followed what was perceived as the custom of the Vilna
Gaon.

Hasidim and the Prohibition of gebrochts
Another stringent custom which the Hasidim adopted—in the opinion of many, unnecessarily—was the
prohibition of eating *gebrochts* (cooked food) on Passover. The Talmud cites an opinion in the name of R. Meir
that it is possible to fulfill the mitzvah of eating matzah
on Passover, i.e., the matzah which is eaten at the First
Seder, with matzah which has been soaked in water or
fruit juice. This opinion is cited in the Shulhan Arukh:
"One may fulfill one's obligation with matzah which has
been soaked, so long as it has not disintegrated."[39] It is
clear, therefore, that *there is no prohibition of gebrochts at
all.* As Wertheim pointed out, "a new rule[40] has spread
among Hasidim . . . , *nearly* all without exception were

extremely careful not to eat matzah which has come in contact with water all of Passover, aside from the last day—the eighth day—of Passover (outside the land of Israel, of course), on which they allow themselves to eat *gebrochts*."[41]

This stringency became more popular in the wake of a responsum of R. Shneur Zalman of Liady (1747–1812), the father of Habad Hasidism, who dwelled on this matter at great length.

> Indeed, even though there is no absolute prohibition and it is clear[ly allowed] within the strict meaning of the law (*barur mi-dina*), one who wishes to be stringent will be blessed, and he is not to be considered a fool who holds to a meaningless stringency. Rather there is a great reason behind this— to distance oneself from any shadow of a violation of a Torah-prohibition.[42]

In explaining the reason for this in detail, he emphasizes that:

> We have seen with our own eyes that many matzot have a little flour on them even after the baking. This happens because the flour, which was not well-kneaded originally, contained hard lumps . . . and it is impossible to deny the evidence of our senses. The reason that the Poskim have not mentioned this is because it is not common except in hard dough which has not been kneaded thoroughly. In recent generations they would spend a good

deal of time kneading the dough until it was thoroughly done—until *some twenty years ago or more, [the custom] of taking great care in kneading the dough quickly [so that it would not become leavened in the process] has spread among the holy ones of Israel, and so the kneading is not done thoroughly.* And so we find a little flour in matzot made out of hard dough [i.e., dough not kneaded thoroughly], as is visible to those who are truly exacting in this matter.

Now this real flour which remains on the surface of the matzah may become leavened (*hametz*) when the matzah is crumbled into the soup, as is commonly done on Shabbat, and there is thus a true concern of leavening even according to Torah law, for this is not merely a mixture of *hametz* [but true unmixed *hametz*]. [And] according to that which the Arizal wrote, that we should be strict in regard to every stringency on Passover, it is clear that we should be strict in this matter as well. . . . Nevertheless, one who wishes to be lenient in this matter on the last day of Passover because of concern for the joy of the holiday has not lost anything thereby. As far as [kneading with] fruit juice is concerned, it is clear that there is no reason to be strict.

From R. Shneur Zalman's description we might conclude that this stringency was but twenty years old in his time, but that is not so. On the contrary, we find the Gaon R. Yaakov Emden citing his father, the Hakham Tzvi Ashkenazi (1660–1718), who wrote: "Regarding matzah which has been soaked, some people, who wish to be thought of as pious, keep far from it, but he [= the Hakham Tzvi], may his memory be for a blessing, refuted all the arguments of these would-be pious ones."[43] From this we may conclude that already a century before R. Shneur Zalman there were "would-be pious ones [who] kept from matzah which had been soaked."

More than that, we find that there were those who prohibited it for themselves even in the time of the Rishonim, as we see from the fact that the custom is mentioned by the Raavan, R. Eliezer b. Nathan (ca. 1090–1170) of Mainz in the Rhineland in Germany, one of the first Tosafists.

> Matzah which has been baked and is then cooked . . . cannot become leavened, and is permitted. *There are those who do not wish to soak the matzah in soup during the first night,* for they see that this is what their fathers did, and they think that it was so that the matzah would not become leavened, but this is not so. [Their fathers] followed this custom [of not soaking the matzot during the first seder] in order that the taste of the matzah should not depart from their mouths.[44]

However, as noted, R. Shneur Zalman gave another reason for this prohibition, and tied it to the change which had occurred some twenty years before. This would naturally explain why the prohibition had not been mentioned by earlier Poskim.

Later Aharonim tried hard to refute R. Shneur Zalman's arguments and permit *gebrochts altogether;* see the long discussion of R. Hayyim Mordekhai Margoliot in *Shaarei Teshuvah*, O.H. 460:10. The Vilna Gaon laid down the operative rule (*halakhah le-maaseh*) to cook matzah on Passover and make kneidlach (dumplings), for even if we fear that some (unbaked) flour has been left within the matzah, whatever is in a hot oven does not become leavened. And so we find in *Minhat Yehudah* of R. Yehudah Halevi Epstein (Warsaw, 5638).

> Our Master of the Exile, the Gaon R. Hayyim Volozhin, once went during the intermediate days of Passover to visit his teacher, the Vilna Gaon, to see if he ate kneidlach. The Vilna Gaon ate them in his presence and said that there was no reason to be concerned [i.e., about violating any prohibition, even tangentially]. This is especially so for those who cook them in boiling water. [Now,] when [the kneidlach] are made with goose fat without water, then even the unbaked flour [which remains] is permitted—and certainly if it is afterwards cooked in boiling water.[45]

Even the Hatam Sofer was lenient in the matter of *gebrochts,* as R. Shimon Greenfield reports.[46] In our generation, R. Ovadiah Yosef ruled permissively as well. However, the Hasidim do not follow those who wish to be lenient in this, since they follow their teachers in being strict.

The Matter of Kitniyot

Since we are dealing with customs touching on Pass-over, what better example of the ways of stringency is there than the story of kitniyot.[47] The development of this prohibition has been described in detail by R. S. I. Zevin in his important volume, Ha-Moadim ba-Hala-khah.[48] There is no reason to repeat his discussion; here I will merely sum things up. The prohibition appears first at the turn of the thirteenth century in France, in the *Semak* of R. Yehudah of Corbeil,[49] as a custom which some of the Sages of his time followed. And even the *Mordekhai*, composed by the *Semak*'s brother-in-law, reports that R. Yehiel of Paris would eat white beans on Passover.[50] In the Tur the prohibition appears in the name of "some prohibit," but the Tur concludes that this is an unnecessary stringency, and "we do not follow it."[51] The Rema, in his *Darkei Moshe*, adds that "we Ashkenazim are accustomed to be stringent [in this]."[52] This stringency was certainly adopted under the influ-ence of the Maharil and his following. The custom became so widespread in Germany that R. Israel Isserlin, the author of *Terumat ha-Deshen*, was once asked whether "crops of legumes . . . upon which water had fallen and it is close to certain that they have become leavened may be stored away during Passover, or not?" His decision was permissive.[53] We also find the prohibi-tion of products made from legumes mentioned in his work, particularly oil, for he permitted burning oil made from legumes, since the prohibition was limited to eating and deriving benefit from such products was not included.

The question of baking matzot from the flour of legumes became a particularly difficult issue. Surprisingly, despite the clear and widely accepted opinion of the Rambam that legumes have no leavening in them,[54] a long line of Poskim prohibited it, "for how can one imagine . . . permitting that which earlier authorities prohibited?"[55]

Despite this, the Poskim explain that "kitniyos" do not prohibit a dish if the flour falls into a pot, even when the usual measure of sixty times the amount of permitted substance is not present to neutralize the prohibited substance;[56] one should only toss out what is visible.[57] Nevertheless, still later authorities have decided that the custom is not so lenient, and sixty times the prohibited substance is necessary in order to permit the dish for eating. This applies to the pots in which the legume-tainted dish was cooked; though the essential rule permits one to eat from them on Passover, and even on the same day, nevertheless, "people have become accustomed to be strict in this matter, and in cases where [parents] cook legumes for small children, they use special cooking utensils [which are not used for adults]."[58]

There has also been a steadily widening definition of what species of legumes are included in the prohibition, to the point that the botanical definition has become irrelevant, and even species which merely resemble legumes, grow like them, or are used to produce food products similar to those made from legumes, have become prohibited. Some have wanted to prohibit potatoes and potato flour because of "kitniyos."[59]

This air of stringency has proceeded to the point that some have prohibited the legumes themselves, and not only flour made from them, something for which there would seem to be no basis whatsoever.[60] This prohibition would apply with greater force than those adopted in the case of the grains used for matzah, for those who prohibit do so even when those who produce flour from legumes observe the eighteen-minute rule, do not use salt, etc.[61] In recent years the prohibition of "kitniyos" has been extended to the area of mixtures as well, as is clear from the various "Passover guides" that have been published.

Notes

1. *Minhagei Yisrael*, vol. 1, pp. 92–97, and vol. 2, pp. 141–149.
2. Matzah kept from contact with water from the time of the harvesting of the wheat from which it is made.
3. Or: guard or watch.
4. Scarcity or some other serious difficulty.
5. See below.
6. O.H. 453:4.
7. See Menahot 53a, where it is clear that even in the Temple, the meal-offerings, which are equated in this respect with matzah, were guarded from the time of kneading only; see also Pesahim 40a; Mekilta deRashbi, ed. Epstein-Melamed, p. 22; Mishnah Pesahim 3:4 (Bavli Pesahim 48b, Yerushalmi Shabbat 7:2 [28b]).

   However, there is a contrary view expressed in the sources, one which requires guarding from the beginning;

see further on in Pesahim 40a, and Tosafot there, s.v. *ki*, the collection of Geonic responsa named *Shaarei Teshuvah*, no. 30, and see the next note.

8. See *Sefer ha-Manhig*, Dinei Matzah, siman 41, ed. Refael, pp. 460–461; Hulin 7b, Rashi, s.v. *dibe-mitzvah*; *Sefer ha-Orah*, p. 188; *Sefer ha-Pardes*, p. 127, ed. Ehrenreich, p. 41; *Siddur Rashi*, siman 368, p. 179; *Mahzor Vitry*, siman 18, p. 259; *Shibbolei ha-Leket*, siman 210, p. 170, in the name of "Hilkhot Pesah le-Rabbenu Shelomo."

9. Perek 2, siman 26, cited in the Tur, O.H. 453. In this connection, see J. Maendel, "The 'French' Mill in Mediaeval Tuscany," *Journal of Mediaeval History* 14 (1982): 215–247.

10. See Shulhan Arukh there, where the commentators note that in the time of the Talmud a hand mill was used, and so there was no water involved; later on, when water mills came into use, the guarding had to begin from the time of grinding.

11. See She'iltot to Tzav, siman 90 (ed. Mirsky, siman 90, pp. 49–50).

12. See Rashi on Pesahim 40a, s.v. *umi-mai*. Some hold that even when water falls on the harvested wheat, the wheat is still permitted as long as it is not moist and its appearance has not changed, nor has it softened (see Meiri to Pesahim 40a, ed. Klein, p. 129, in accordance with the Geonic Responsa *Shaarei Teshuvah*, nos. 95 and 293, cited by the *Ittur*, Matzah u-Maror, p. 129a, and Tur-Shulhan Arukh, O.H. 467). However, the Meiri notes his own hesitation on the matter because of the difficulty of examining the kernels, and recommends buying wheat and guarding it for Passover use, and even more so from the time of harvesting (see also *Sefer ha-Pardes* of Rashi, siman 149).

13. See my article in *Sidra* 4b (1988): 163–164.

14. That is, the reading the Gemara can be either מצה or מצוה. On the difference between the two, see the illuminating

remarks of R. M. M. Kasher in *Torah Shelemah* on Bo, p. 153.

15. The exact definition of this term is a matter of dispute between Rishonim; see Rashi, Pesahim 40a, s.v. *umi-mai*, who suggests that it refers to sometime "before this" (= kneading); Tosafot there, s.v. *ki*, who suggest that this is when it is still *dagan*, "corn," i.e., wheat after threshing; and *Shaarei Teshuvah* 95, where the need for watching is "from beginning to end."

16. *Sefer ha-Orah*, siman 84, p. 94.

17. Netiv Hamishi, pt. 4. This is the case even though Rabbenu Yeruham himself decided in favor of the opinion of the Sages of Germany and France, i.e., that from the time of kneading is the most crucial. He thus agreed with the position of the Tosafists that the requirement of guarding from the harvest is a *humra*. See n. 12 above where Meiri is cited.

18. O.H. 453.

19. See *Halamish* 4 (1986): 30–31.

20. *Res Rustica* II, chap. 18, pars. 1–2.

21. See most recently the responsa *Shaarei Yeshua* of R. Yeshua Shababo Yedia Zein (the author of *Porat Shushan*) (Jerusalem, 5748), shaar 6, siman 4, pp. 86–87, where the author discusses the question of whether this is a stringency close to the actual law, or whether it is a mere custom which only Ashkenazim, whose ancestors accepted it, are obliged to maintain (see there, p. 85).

22. *Sefer Maharil*, ed. S. Y. Spitzer (Jerusalem, 5749), Hilkhot Afiyyat Matzah, siman 1, p. 60.

23. He died in 5553.

24. *Responsa Noda Bi-Yehudah Tinyana*, siman 79.

25. See *Hayyei Adam*, by one of the Vilna Gaon's closest disciples, R. Avraham Danzig, kelal 128, siman 30.

26. See A. Wertheim, *Hilkhot va-Halikhot ba-Hasidut* (Jerusalem, 5720), p. 172; in English, *Laws and Customs in Hasidism*

(Hoboken, N.J., 1992), p. 258.

27. Wertheim, p. 171 (English, p. 259). Only the Habad Hasidim (Lubavitchers) were somewhat less strict in this, relying on the Shulhan Arukh of the Alter Rebbe, the Baal HaTanya, who wrote in O.H. 453:19 that "Israel is all holy, and Jews guard all the matzot of the Passover holiday from the time of *grinding onward*. . . . But it is proper to be strict about the wheat which is used for the mitzvah-matzah itself, if it is possible, from the time of reaping." Among Lubavitcher Hasidim, the custom is to be strict in regard to the first Seder (Wertheim, p. 172 [English: p. 258]).

In Eretz Israel the custom was also to keep the wheat from water from the time of reaping; see *Minhagei Eretz Yisrael* of R. Y. Gelles (Jerusalem, 5728), pp. 128–129, siman 24, who cites the sources. There were also *mehadrin* who followed the view of the Rambam and ate such matzah all of Passover. This was true as well of the Jews of Libya; see *Korot Luv vi-Yehudeha . . . "Higid Mordekhai"*, ed. H. Goldberg (Jerusalem, 5742), p. 184. It was also the custom of individuals in other places.

28. See Wertheim, pp. 200, 172 (English: pp. 302, 258).

29. See his comments at the end of Pesahim, *Orhot Hayyim*, Hilkhot Sukkah, siman 34 (p. 249); Ibn Ezra, Hizkuni, and others.

30. See Shulhan Arukh, O.H. 475:6.

31. *Maaseh Rav*, siman 185; see *Maaseh Rav ha-Shalem*, ed. R. M. Zlushinksky (Jerusalem, 5747), pp. 208–209.

32. *Responsa Meshiv Davar*, Y.D., siman 77.

33. Vol. 2, siman 275.

34. In his responsa, vol. 1, siman 209.

35. Y.D., siman 191.

36. See *Maaseh Rav*, loc. cit. Several of the editor's references should be corrected.

37. *Sedei Hemed*, vol. 8, pp. 466 f. (Hametz u-Matzah 14:6).
38. Maharsham, loc. cit.
39. Pesahim 41a. See *Mishnah Berurah* 461, n. 17, that this rule is only *di'avad* (*post-factum*), but that those who are unable to eat dry matzah, such as the old or the sick, are permitted to eat such matzah *lekhathillah* (*ab initio*). See also n. 18 there regarding the differences in this regard between soaking and cooking, between water and fruit juice, etc.
40. To be exact, not entirely new; see below.
41. Aaron Wertheim, *Law and Custom in Hasidism*, Hoboken: Ktav, 1992, p. 261.
42. Responsum 6 at the end of *Shulhan Arukh ha-Rav* 5, p. 892a–b.
43. *She'ilat Yaavetz* 2, siman 68.
44. Pesahim 39a, ed. R. S. Z. Ehrenreich (Zemlui, 5696), p. 162a. See *Shaar Ha-Tziyyun* to O.H. 461:29.
45. See *Maaseh Rav ha-Shalem*, ed. R. Mordekhai Zlotshinski (Jerusalem, 5747), siman 187, n. 3, pp. 211–212; and Responsa *Yehavveh Daat* of R. Ovadiah Yosef (Jerusalem, 5737), vol. 1, siman 21, p. 63.
46. See *Responsa Maharshag* (Varnov, 5691), vol. 1, siman 56; see *Yehavveh Daat* there. As to the view of the Hazon Ish, see R. Yoel Schwartz in his *Hametz Mashehu* (Jerusalem, 5748), p. 64, that the Hazon Ish was not particular about this, except that he would soak matzah in fruit juice or boiling water, since there was no danger of leavening.
47. Pp. 255–262.
48. (Tel Aviv, 1957), pp. 255–262.
49. Siman 223.
50. See *Mordekhai*, Pesahim, chap. 2, siman 588.
51. O.H. 453.
52. Ibid.
53. Siman 113.
54. Hilkhot Hametz u-Matzah 5:1.

55. R. Mordekhai Zeev Ettinga, Responsa *Maamar Mordekhai* (Lvov, 5612), siman 32. See Zevin, pp. 260–261.

56. See *Beer Hetev* to O.H. 453:2, who cites the *Hok Yaakov*, and see Zevin, p. 258; see also R. S. Z. Grossman, *Siddur Pesah ke-Hilkhato*, vol. 1, pp. 187–188, and in *Yesodei Yeshurun*, pp. 414–415.

57. *Hayyei Adam* 127:1.

58. See R. Yoel Schwartz, *Hametz be-Mashehu*, p. 58, and *Siddur Pesah ke-Hilkhato*, pp. 186–187.

59. See R. S. Z. Grossman, *Siddur Pesah ke-Hilkhato*, vol. 1, pp. 182–186. R. Yaakov Emden, *She'ilat Yaavetz*, vol. 2, siman 65, opposed this in the name of his father, and see *Sedei Hemed* 8, p. 239a, and *Yesodei Yeshurun*, pp. 422–423. Even some Sephardim have advocated adopting these Ashkenazic stringencies, a move strongly opposed by R. Ovadiah Yosef; see, aside from the source quoted above in *Yehavveh Daat, Hazon Ovadiah*, vol. 2, p. 63, and in the Milluim, pp. 295 f., *Responsa Yabia Omer*, vol. 1, Y.D. 3. In all of this he distinguishes between personal stringencies and those which affect the community. Though Sephardic scholars may adopt the first, they are forbidden to rule stringently for others in their communities.

60. *Siddur Pesah ke-Hilkhato*, p. 186.

61. Ibid., "and so is the custom"; see n. 29 there.

PART III
MINOR OCCASIONS

CHAPTER 6[1]
Taanit Bahab (בה״ב)[2]

IT IS THE CUSTOM in Germany and France to fast the Monday, Thursday, and Monday after the festivals of Passover and Sukkot, [though] they wait until the entire months of Nisan and Tishrei have passed before fasting, since they do not wish to fast during those months [which are generally joyous times]. They rely on the verse in Job for this: "When the days of feasting came round, [Job sent and sanctified them, rose early in the morning and offered burnt offerings for each, for Job thought] perhaps my children have sinned [and blasphemed in their hearts. So was Job's custom all his life.]"[3]

The Tur explains that "since these are days of feasting and joy, perhaps [someone was led to] sin."[4]

It would seem that the Tur's reason originates in a Tosafist explanation for a phrase which appears in Kiddushin, "the sorest spot of the year is the festival," regarding the day after a festival (Isru Hag).[5] That is, "they are days of the year [in which men and women] stay together in private and [in which] sin [may thus occur], i.e., the days of the festival in which there are groups of men and women [who come] to hear the sermon and look at one other. Some say this is the reason for the custom of fasting after Passover and after Sukkot."[6]

A similar reason is given in *Orhot Hayyim*, Hilkhot Taanit, siman 1 (p. 206), where the danger of feasting is emphasized; because of the excessive eating, drinking, and rejoicing associated with the festival, people become looser in their behavior, and the fasts atone for that.[7]

However, this is not the only reason given in the sources for the custom. It also does not explain why there is no Bahab after Shavuot, as the *Mordekhai* notes, "we do not find people fasting [after Shavuot] *anywhere*." The *Beit Yosef* attempts to answer this objection by pointing out that Shavuot is only a day or two, and so there is not so much opportunity or motivation for loose behavior.[8] However, this answer is not convincing, since the threat of sin is present even in one or two days of feasting. After all, the Talmud records the conversation of the prophet Elijah with R. Yehudah the brother of R. Sala Hasida. "Why does the Messiah not come?" "[Why?] Because even this very day, Yom Kippur, several virgins have been deflowered in Nehardea!"[9]

Yet another reason is given in *Mahzor Vitry*: "After Passover, starting from Rosh Hodesh Iyyar, the people of the exile are accustomed to declare three fasts, and so too after Sukkot from Marheshvan they fast Monday, Thursday, Monday. [On these days] *they temper the days of our exile*, recite Selihot, and read Vayehal Moshe from the Torah with three *aliyot*. During Minhah they recite the Haftarah of Dirshu Hashem BeHimatz'o—*Bet*[10] *Heh*[11] *mitzu*."[12] *Mahzor Vitry* thus derives a hint of these fasts from the Haftarah for a fast itself.

The Maharil suggests yet another reason, deriving the custom from another verse: "Serve God with joy, and rejoice with trembling."[13] "Where there is joy there should be trembling—that is, fasting."[14] He also cites the verse from Job which the Tur mentions; see above.

The *Mordekhai*'s observation that these fasts are not observed after Shavuot does not apply universally; the Raavad of Posquières records threefold fasts for each of the three festivals,[15] as does R. Aharon of Lunel in his *Orhot Hayyim*.[16] Both of these reflect a Provençal background; evidently southern France differed from the north in this respect. There is even a hint of the remnants of this custom in Eretz Israel, in the *piyyut* of a contemporary of the *Beit Yosef*, the Yemenite Yahya al-Sahari.[17]

There is also a dispute regarding the start of these fasts after Sukkot. Mahari Weil ruled that they are not to start until 17 Marheshvan, in case the first rains in Eretz Israel are delayed, and he cites the Ravyah and Maharil in support.[18] The Shakh too connects these fasts with the possible delay of the vital rains in Eretz Israel, but in doing so, dates the start somewhat earlier, to the seventh of the month.[19]

We must seriously consider that this disagreement concerns not only the date of the onset of the fasts, but the reason for them as well. Indeed, *Sefer Hasidim* explicitly rejects the "sinful" reason:

> The reason for fasting after Passover and Sukkot is not because they have sinned . . . but these fasts are *for rain*. In Marheshvan they fast during the first week . . . in order that the Yoreh should fall on the seeds in a blessed way, and in Iyyar in order that [the crops] not be struck with blight or rot. Therefore they read the Torah as the Rishonim used to do in order that rain descend in a beneficial way.[20]

The *Beit Yosef*, in his discussion of this custom, included this reason as well, precisely in order to explain why the northern French custom did not include Shavuot.[21] "It seems to me that we follow the custom of the Babylonians in every case, and they fast after Sukkot when the first rains do not fall, and the Ninevites do so after Passover, as the Yerushalmi notes that the inhabitants of Nineveh must fast after Passover, but we do not find [the custom of] fasting after Shavuot anywhere."[22] The opinion of the Ravyah—that the reason for these fasts is because of concern for rain—is cited in the *Beit Yosef* as transmitted by the *Mordekhai*.

An additional reason is found in the *Levush*, one which explains the need for the fasts after Shavuot also. R. Mordekhai Yaffe suggests that the change of seasons brings a change in "air," which could be injurious to people's health, and so they fast to prevent this.[23]

We see therefore that European communities fasted in case the rains in Eretz Israel had been delayed—another instance illustrating the close connection between Europe and Eretz Israel, a connection and influence which shows up in innumerable ways.[24]

However, this suggestion does not explain the fasts after Passover. For this we need another proposal, which separates the fasts after Passover from those after Sukkot. In Eretz Israel they fasted Taanit Esther three days *after* Purim (Shulhan Arukh, O.H. 686:2). This custom is documented in Masekhet Soferim 17:2:[25] "The three days of the Fast [of Purim] are not fasted one after the other, but on separate days, Monday, Thursday, Monday, and *our teachers in Eretz Israel* have been accustomed to fast after Purim. . . . *Moreover, we delay punishment [= the fast] and do not advance it.*"

Why fast in Adar, then? After all, Esther's fast was in Nisan, on Passover! Masekhet Soferim takes up this issue as well, "Why do we not fast in Nisan? Because the Mishkan was set up on the first day of the month . . . and so in future times it will be [re]built in Nisan. . . .

Therefore we do not say Tahanun all that month, and we do not fast *until Nisan is over*."[26]

Masekhet Soferim is like a mosaic, with its pieces coming from various places and times. Some of its teachings reflect "the custom of our teachers in Eretz Israel," some "our teachers in the West," etc. In our case, it seems that there were two customs reflected in these halakhot: one in which the three days of Taanit Esther fell at the end of the month of Adar, as close to Purim as possible, and one in which the three days fell in Iyyar, so as not to impinge on the joyousness of the month of Nisan, and so as not to advance the fast but to delay it. There seems to have been a third custom, where the three fasts *were* fulfilled during Nisan, a custom commented on favorably by *Sefer Hasidim*.[27]

If this suggestion is correct, what happened was as follows. In the course of time, when the Babylonian custom of fasting only one day for Taanit Esther, on 13 Adar, took hold, the three-day Eretz Israel custom of fasting in Adar, Nisan, or Iyyar was forgotten.[28] Thus, there is no connection with the fasts after Sukkot and those after Passover; they were followed for different reasons. The three after Sukkot came for fear of delaying the rains, and the three after Passover were connected to Purim. There was no reason for fasting after Shavuot, and so no one did. However, once the original reasons for these fasts were forgotten, with the transfer of Taanit Esther to one day in Adar, other reasons were given to explain them in a unified manner—for atonement. In

Provence, the fasts after Shavuot stemmed from a desire for symmetry.

Unfortunately, the matter is not so simple. For there is a Geonic responsum which is attributed to R. Paltoi Gaon, which describes the custom of the Suran yeshiva in Babylonia as *"fasts of after the week of the Festival,"* emphasizing that Vayehal must be read as for any other public fast,[29] and which does not differentiate between festivals—these fasts seem to have followed each of the three festivals. Moreover, since he mentions the Fast of Purim separately, the post-Passover fasts are not to be confused with them. Indeed, they seem to have fallen at the end of Adar—an Eretz Israel custom in the heart of Babylonian Jewry!

We must seriously consider that it is this custom which lies behind the Provençal custom which is mentioned by the Raabad and *Orhot Hayyim*, and which included a post-Shavuot series of fasts. And since the Geonim do not reveal the reason for these fasts, we may perhaps follow the reason given by the Rishonim, that these fasts were set for atonement following the rejoicing of the festivals.

To summarize, we have seen an instructive process whereby two independent developments appear to combine. According to the Babylonian custom, there are three sets of fasts, one after each festival, while according to the Ashkenazic custom, which follows that of Eretz Israel, Bahab after Passover is really a delayed Taanit Esther, while those after Sukkot were set over concern for delayed rains. In the course of time and due to several factors, the reasons for the Eretz Israel customs were forgotten, and the Babylonian reasons were melded onto them. However, the question of why there were no post-Shavuot fasts then arose. This question gave rise to various additional reasons, which added an additional layer of unclarity to the issue of the origin of these customs.

Notes

1. *Minhagei Yisrael*, vol. 1, pp. 192–199.
2. "Monday, Thursday, Monday"; see immediately below.
3. Job 1:5, see Tur, O.H. 492.
4. Ibid.
5. Kiddushin 81a.
6. Tosafot Kiddushin 81, s.v. *sakva*.
7. So too in the *Kolbo*, Hilkhot Taanit, siman 1, in the same words as *Orhot Hayyim*. These works also record a more stringent custom: fasting every Monday and Thursday from Passover to Shavuot, and from Sukkot to Hanukkah. *Orhot Hayyim* adds three more to the months of Marheshvan and Iyyar.
8. *Beit Yosef*, O.H. 429; so too the *Levush*, O.H. 492.
9. Yoma 19b.
10. That is, Day 2 = Monday.
11. That is, Day 5 = Thursday.
12. See *Mahzor Vitry*, siman 285, p. 310.
13. Psalms 2:11.
14. *Minhagim*, Seder Sheni va-Hamishi ve-Sheni (Jerusalem, 5729), p. 201a.
15. *Temim De'im*, siman 177.
16. Hilkhot Taanit.

17. See R. S. H. Kook, *Iyyunim u-Mehqarim*, vol. 2 (Jerusalem, 5723), p. 25.
18. Mahari Weil, *Dinim va-Halakhot*, siman 14; see *Sefer Ravyah*, Minhagim, Hilkhot Shabbat Bereshit, p. 56b and siman 849, vol. 3, pp. 594–595; see n. 2 there.
19. Y.D. 220, n. 31. The seventh of the month is mentioned in the Mishnah; see Taanit 1:4.
20. *Sefer Hasidim*, ed. Margaliot, pp. 204–205.
21. *Beit Yosef*, O.H. 429.
22. *Beit Yosef*, O.H. 629.
23. See R. R. Margaliot's *Nefesh Hayyah* (Tel Aviv, 5714), to O.H. 492, p. 108, where he suggests still another reason.
24. There is a large body of scholarship on this topic; see the important book of A. Grossman, *Hakhmei Ashkenaz ha-Rishonim* (Jerusalem, 5741), pp. 424–434, where he summarizes the opinions on this. See also the review of Y. Ta-Shema in *Kiryat Sefer* 56 (5741): 345–348, as well as the later comments in *Asufot* 2 (5748): 177 f., and *Kiryat Sefer* 60 (5745): 306–309, as well as *Sidra* 3 (5747): 155–156.
25. Ed. Higger, p. 25.
26. Soferim 21:1, ed. Higger, p. 353.
27. Ed. Wistinetzki, siman 67, p. 44.
28. See below, chap, 11, n. 19.
29. See *Hemdah Genuzah*, siman 4.

PART IV
SEFIRAH

CHAPTER 7[1]
"Leshem Yihud" Before
Counting the Omer

IN THE SIDDUR PUBLISHED ORIGINALLY by R. Yaakov Emden, current editions contain the following version of the Bakashah ("Request, Entreaty") which is recited before the counting of the Omer:[2]

לשם יחוד . . . הנני מוכן ומזומן לקיים מצות עשה של ספירת העומר.
כמו שכתוב . . . תספרו חמישים יום (והקרבתם מנחה חדשה לה').[3]

Why were the last four words enclosed in parentheses? Were they to be deleted? After all, we have the principle that "we are not permitted to divide the verse in a way which does not have Sinaitic warrant."[4]

However, it is known that these words do not appear in other siddurim; so too they are not in the prayer of Ribbono shel Olam which is recited after the counting.

The latter issue has been dealt with by the Aharonim: "This is apparently a separate mitzvah and does not relate to the counting of the Omer, as is noted in *Iyyun Tefillah*. Even the Ribbono shel Olam which is recited after the counting ends the verse in the middle with תספרו חמישים יום. Perhaps there it is recited as part of a prayer and may therefore be divided, as *Nishmat Adam* notes in kelal 5."[5]

Therefore, it seems that despite the general rule of not dividing a Biblical verse, the ones who formulated these prayers did so, and the Emden Siddur reflects the hesitation of its editors as to whether to include the end of the verse or not. As a compromise, they put parentheses around the end. However, the basic issue remains: why did the ones who composed the prayer end their quotation of the verse in the middle?

The solution to this riddle may be found in the policy adopted in *Siddur ha-Shelah*, where it is emphasized that Psalms 91 should be recited prior to retiring for the night only up to the middle of verse 10—making exactly sixty words. This follows the Talmudic statement in Shevuot 15b, where this passage is recommended.[6] The Abudarham explains this as corresponding to the sixty words in Birkat Kohanim, together with Song of Songs

3:7, "Sixty warriors did Solomon have."[7]

Now, the number forty-nine plays a large role in the counting of the Omer, for obvious reasons. So too has the custom arisen to recite Psalms 67 before the counting, because this mizmor contains, aside from the heading in the first verse, seven verses and forty-nine words. Each word in this mizmor is taken to refer to one of the days of the counting. Likewise, there is a custom to recite Ana Be-Koah after the counting, a prayer which also has seven verses, each corresponding to one of the weeks of the count.[8]

Returning to our problem, the number of words in the version of Le-Shem Yihud which we cited above is forty-nine—without the words in parentheses, corresponding to the forty-nine days of the counting. It may therefore be that which caused the ones who compiled the prayer to end the verse in the middle.

Notes

1. *Minhagei Yisrael*, vol. 1, pp. 98–100.
2. P. 259. It should be noted that this Bakashah is not found in the original Emden Siddur, *Amudei Shammayim* I and *Shaarei Shammayim* II, published at Altona, 5505–5507, vol. 2, p. 53b. This addition first appears in the Lemberg edition of 5664, as is noted in the list of additions to the second part, p. 3. Regarding the siddur *Beit Yaakov*, see the editor's introduction to the facsimile edition of *Amudei Shammayim*, 5723, pp. 1–2.
3. Leviticus 23:15–16.
4. See Berakhot 12b, Taanit 27b, Megillah 22a, *Magen*

Avraham to O.H. 422:8, *Nishmat Adam*, Kelal 5, siman 2. See
above Chapter 3 pp. 32–36.
5. R. Yisrael Hayyim Friedmann, *Likkutei ha-Maharih Friedmann*, vol. 3 (Marmarosh-Siget, 5660), p. 33a.
6. Though our texts of the Talmud have the end of verse 10
in parentheses, Talmudic manuscripts and the Rishonim
do not; see *Dikdukei Soferim* there, n. *tzaddi*.
7. See *Abudarham ha-Shalem* (Jerusalem, 5723), p. 33. This prescription is also found in the Ritva to Shevuot.
8. See S. Tal, *Peri Hayyim* (Tel Aviv, 5723), pp. 77–78, and
what he wrote there, pp. 30–32. Cf above Chapter 2, p. 23.

CHAPTER 8[1]
The Customs of Mourning During the Counting of the Omer

THE SHULHAN ARUKH lays down the following rule:

> It is the custom not to have one's hair cut until Lag Be-Omer, for it is said that [the disciples of R. Akiva] then ceased to die. . . . [In paragraph 3, the author adds:] And some have the custom of having their hair cut on Rosh Hodesh Iyyar, and that is an error.[2]

On this latter comment, the Rema notes:

> However, in many places the custom is to [allow] haircutting until Rosh Hodesh Iyyar, and [people in] those [places] should not have their hair cut from Lag Be-Omer onward. . . . And [people] in those [places in which] the custom is to cut one's hair from Lag Be-Omer onward should not have their hair cut at all after Passover until Lag Be-Omer.

From this we may see that there were two different customs: the Sephardic custom, which R. Yosef Karo cites, which holds that the prohibition of hair cutting, and the customs of mourning, are in effect from Passover until Lag Be-Omer, and the custom of "many places" in Ashkenaz, where the mourning period is begun only with Rosh Hodesh Iyyar, but continues until Shavuot.

Let us investigate how these two customs developed.

As is known, they both have their origin in the report in Talmudic sources regarding the twelve thousand pairs of disciples of R. Akiva who died of croup between Passover and Shavuot because they did not treat each other respectfully.[3]

R. Isaac Giat comments on this that "from that time the custom arose to mourn them."[4] According to this opinion, then, the custom should be not to have one's hair cut all through the period between Passover and Shavuot, for it was then that the disciples of R. Akiva died. Indeed, this was the Geonic custom, for R. Isaac Giat himself writes that "the custom in all Israel is not to marry from Passover to Shavuot. This is for reasons of mourning and not [halakhic] prohibition (*issur*), for so have the Sages reported: 'Twelve thousand. . .' [The custom] of not marrying during this period . . . began that year."[5]

In the Geonic *Halakhot Pesuqot* we find, among the responsa of Rav Natronai Gaon, the following excerpt:

> Regarding that which you have asked: Why we do not betroth or marry women in these days, whether this is because of a prohibition (*issur*) or not? Be

aware that this is not because of a prohibition, but rather because of a custom of mourning, for Hazal said: "R. Akiva had twelve thousand pairs of disciples all of whom died between Passover and Shavuot." And from that time onward the earlier authorities established the custom not to marry on those [days].[6]

Rabbenu Yeruham reports the same custom in the name of Rav Hai Gaon.[7] However, an additional custom associated with this event is reported in his name in other works of the Rishonim.[8]

Regarding [the tradition] that people are accustomed not to do any work from sunset to the morning, this is because of the disciples of R. Akiva, who died after sunset and were buried after sunset, and so people refrained from work [in their honor]. Moreover, it is written, "seven complete weeks shall there be," with the word *shabbat* used for "week," [thus connecting this with the word] *shevut*, which denotes a "cessation" [from work] and a "cessation" [from economic activity, as implied by a similar use of the word *shabbat* in connection] with the sabbatical year: "seven weeks of years." Just as agricultural work is prohibited during the sabbatical year, so too during the counting of the Omer; namely, after sunset we cease from work.

Thus the two primary characteristics of the period in Geonic times were both carried out for the entire period from Passover to Shavuot.

However, R. Avraham b.R. Nathan ha-Yarhi, in his *Sefer ha-Manhig*, reports that

> the custom in France and Provence is to marry from Lag Be-Omer onward. I heard in the name of R. Zerahiah Gerondi, who found in an old manuscript found in Spain, that [the disciples of R. Akiva] died from Passover until *peros* Shevuot. What is *pursa*? "Half," as we learned, "They ask [questions] regarding the halakhot of Passover for thirty days before Passover."[9] And [that is] fifteen days before Shavuot, and that is Lag Be-Omer.—A.b.N.[10]

This tradition of the Manhig reached R. David Abudarham and from him (?) reached the Tashbetz,[11] and finally Shulhan Arukh, O.H. 493:1, which laid down the rule that "It is the custom not to marry between Passover and Shavuot, [that is], until Lag Be-Omer."

Thus, there was a Spanish-Provençal tradition that the disciples of R. Akiva died only from Passover until fifteen days before Shavuot. The Meiri has a similar tradition, though he specifies that the day on which the deaths ceased was Lag Be-Omer, and thus not exactly fifteen days before Shavuot, "and so it is customary not to fast on that day, and likewise not to marry from Passover to that time."[12] Whatever the exact day, the prohibition of marrying was limited to the shorter time period in line with this tradition. We have yet to hear about anything regarding the custom of not having one's hair cut or the length of time (thirty-three days, however counted) for this prohibition.

However, in the fourteenth-century sermons of R. Joshua Ibn Shueib we find a tradition close to that of the Manhig, but with the addition of the prohibition of hair-cutting: "Similarly, I have heard that in a midrash that 'until *peros* Shavuot'—fifteen days before Shavuot. . . . When you subtract fifteen days from forty-nine, thirty-four remain, that is, thirty-three full days."

Ibn Shueib added the following: "And we shave on the thirty-fourth in the morning, for part of a day is as the whole day [in regard to mourning customs]."[13]

Thus we find the custom of not shaving or cutting hair mentioned, and from there it passed to the *Beit Yosef*. Along these lines the Tur records this prohibition as "the custom of some places not to have one's hair cut, and some cut their hair from Lag Be-Omer onward, for then they ceased to die," and so too in the *Beit Yosef*: "So wrote R. Joshua Ibn Shueib in the sermon for the First Day of Passover, and so is the common custom among us."[14]

This custom appears also in some sources from the thirteenth century, *Orhot Hayyim* of R. Aharon ha-Kohen of Lunel,[15] and *Shibbolei ha-Leqet* of R. Zedekiah b. R. Avraham ha-Rofe,[16] though in the latter there is an interesting variation: "There are places in which the custom is not to cut hair until Lag Be-Omer." There is no doubt that this custom is connected with the deaths of the disciples of R. Akiva, and so here we have a limitation of the period to thirty-three days, either to Lag Be-Omer or to "*peros* Shavuot." In other words, the duration of the prohibition of hair-cutting because of mourning is connected to their deaths, just as the prohibition of marrying is.

After this the Tur limited the prohibition to the time until Lag Be-Omer, as did the *Beit Yosef*, citing R. David Abudarham in the name of Ibn Yarhi, who had it from R. Zerahiah ha-Levi (even though their comments relate primarily, or only, to the prohibition of marrying) and also of R. Joshua Ibn Shueib (who already mentioned the prohibition of shaving).[17]

We may thus understand the view of the Sephardic Sages that gains its expression in the ruling of the Shulhan Arukh, which establishes the prohibition of hair cutting as extending until Lag Be-Omer. But the view of the Sages of Ashkenaz is difficult, for where did the custom of beginning the period with Rosh Hodesh Iyyar originate?

Surely there is place for only two customs, that of the Geonim, according to the plain sense of Talmudic tradition, according to which the prohibition extends from Passover to Shavuot, and that of the Sages of Spain and Provence, which ends the period at Lag Be-Omer. Where does the third custom, that of Ashkenaz, come from!

It would seem that the key to this puzzle is to be found in other Ashkenazic customs which center around the Omer. According to the *Sefer ha-Minhagim deBei Maharam me-Rottenberg*, "it is a custom not to perform marriages between Passover and Shavuot . . . but after Nisan passes we recite the Zulatot [*piyyutim*] each Sabbath, as, for example, אזכרך דודי. אלקים אל דמי לך אל תשקוט ואל תחרש . . . [18] until Shavuot. The Sabbath before Shavuot we say Yizkor for those killed by the Crusaders[19] and say Av Harahamim."[20] In the *Sefer ha-Minhagim* of R. Avraham Klausner, siman 129,[21] "the Zulat of Rosh Hodesh is set aside by the Zulatot between Passover and Shavuot." And later on he reports that "in Mainz, *when Nisan passes*, they say one Zulat every Shabbat until Shavuot." He then specifies the Zulat said each week.

Therefore, we see that from Rosh Hodesh Iyyar until Shavuot, each Shabbat certain *kinot*, known as *zulatot*, were recited. They would also say Yizkor and Av Harahamim. This continued in later centuries, as *Sefer Maharil* records. Generally, both Yizkor and Av Harahamim were recited on the Sabbath before Shavuot.[22] In a note, the recitation of Av Harahamim in the Rhineland is explicitly connected with the martyrs of the First Crusade, *Gezerot Tatnu*.[23]

Against this background we may understand the different character of the Omer customs of Omer in the Middle Ages, as we find in *Sefer Minhag Tov*, siman 61.[24]

> It is a proper custom not to have one's hair cut and not to put on new clothing or any new thing, or to luxuriate in a bathhouse, or cut one's nails after Passover till Shavuot, in honor of the pure and righteous pious ones who sacrificed themselves for the sanctification of God's Name. But on Lag Be-Omer it is permitted to do all these, because of the miracle which occurred then. [However,] from Lag Be-Omer till Shavuot the prohibition remains in force.

Thus additional prohibitions, unknown from the Geonim, were introduced, such as the prohibition against

wearing wear new clothes, luxuriating in a bathhouse, or
cutting one's nails—not as mourning rituals for the disciples of R. Akiva, but in memory of the martyrs of Tatnu.
These customs were accepted within Ashkenazic Judaism, as we learn from *Sefer Yosef Ometz*,[25] regarding the
wearing of new clothes, and from *Leqet Yosher*, regarding
the prohibition of cutting nails during the Omer.[26]

The scope of these Ashkenazic customs was wide,
including prohibitions on wearing new clothing even on
the Sabbath, cutting nails, reciting Zulatot, Yizkor, Av
Harahamim, even when blessing the new month, according to R. Isaac Tyrnau.[27] As is known, Av Harahamim was composed in honor of the martyrs of Tatnu,
as the Magen Avraham wrote regarding the words of the
Rema that "there are places in which it is not recited
when they bless the New Moon, *except* during the days
of Sefirah, because of the persecutions at that time, and
even when a circumcision falls on these Sabbaths it is
said."[28]

Thus these mourning observances are closely tied to
the First Crusade, which affected all the Jewish communities along the Crusaders' path. Communities were
completely destroyed; men, women, and children were
killed in grotesque ways, without mercy.[29] From documents written close to that time we learn the exact dates
on which various Rhineland communities suffered persecution. Most of the massacres took place after Rosh
Hodesh Iyyar. For example, Speyer was attacked on the
eighth of Iyyar and Worms on the twenty-third; Mainz

suffered the same fate on 3 Sivan. The Jewish community of Cologne was massacred on 6 Sivan. Thus the most
intense suffering occurred between Rosh Hodesh Iyyar
and Shavuot, inclusive. It is no wonder that severe
mourning was observed during this period.

Moreover, there were places in which, though they
were lenient regarding the *takkanah* of the Geonim, and
permitted marriages until Rosh Hodesh Iyyar, they nevertheless maintained the customs in all their rigor after
Rosh Hodesh Iyyar, as the *Shibbolei ha-Leqet* notes.[30]

The exact extent of the mourning customs adopted
varied from region to region and community to community. Some saw the entire Sefirah period as one of persecution and mourning; others accepted them only for the
period of persecution in their immediate vicinity.
Perhaps some of the variations in customs may be
explained in this way. The persecutions began in Rouen
in Normandy—certainly during Nisan—and continued
until the conquest of Jerusalem by the crusaders.[31]

In Germany, too, different customs took hold, as is
discussed at length in *Minhagei Maharil*.

> The Maharil would have his *bahurim* not shave from
> Passover until Lag Be-Omer, though some would do
> so in private before Rosh Hodesh Iyyar. And so too
> the Maharan Stein, who lived three parasangs from
> Mainz, would trim his beard before Rosh Hodesh
> Iyyar, before going on to the yeshiva of Mahari Segal
> in Mainz, so that the day that he shaved would not

be noticeable. However, the Maharil himself would not shave trim his beard until Shavuot.[32]

To summarize: the beginning of the observance of mourning during Sefirah is rooted in an old custom of mourning following the Talmudic tradition regarding the deaths of the disciples of R. Akiva, who died between Passover and Shavuot. The Sephardic custom follows this Talmudic tradition exclusively, and constitutes a remembrance of the old custom. The Ashkenazic tradition, however, reflects the tragedy of the persecutions of Tatnu. Blood touched blood; the blood of R. Akiva's disciples is mixed with the blood of the martyrs of Ashkenaz, who sacrificed themselves for the sanctification of God's Name.

ADDENDUM
Justification for Cutting One's Hair on Rosh Hodesh Iyyar

In addition to attacking customs considered to be mistaken, there are also cases in which the Poskim attempt to defend customs and demonstrate that they have some justification. So we find the Rema attempting to explain the origin of the custom of permitting haircuts on Rosh Hodesh Iyyar, a custom which had become widespread in his time.[33] The *Beit Yosef* also wrote:

"There are some who have their hair cut on Rosh Hodesh Iyyar, since [Rosh Hodesh] is considered a festival and no mourning is permitted. But it seems to me that since most people have not adopted this custom, *it is a mistake* on their part.

This error occurred because of the comment attributed to the Tosafists to the effect that the "thirty-three days" refer not to a continuous thirty-three-day count, as we are accustomed to make, but to thirty-three days within the Omer, excluding the seven days of Passover, the seven Sabbaths, and the two days of Rosh Hodesh—sixteen days in all in which mourning customs are not observed. Deducting these sixteen days from the forty-nine days of the Omer, thirty-three days of mourning remain. And since according to this calculation there is no mourning on the days of Rosh Hodesh, people adopted the custom of cutting their hair on Rosh Hodesh Iyyar.

However, this is mistaken, for the Tosafists' comment refers to those who have the custom of not having their hair cut until Shavuot, for in that case they have days to spare [and still can mourn continuously for thirty-three days]. But for us, who mourn for *only* thirty-three days, [with no days to spare,] it is forbidden to have one's hair cut all thirty-three days [of our custom], *including* Rosh Hodesh. And it is certainly forbidden to allow hair cutting all of the month of Nisan until after Rosh Hodesh Iyyar, [beginning the mourning only at that point].

In the Maharil it is written that there are some who are accustomed to have their hair cut all of the month of Nisan, and that some in our communities are accustomed to be lenient in this matter. And so it seems that not one of these customs is [completely] in error.

However, no one should adopt the leniencies of two of them; [if one adopts the custom of hair cutting until Rosh Hodesh Iyyar,] one should not cut one's hair after Lag Be-Omer onward; even if one cuts one's hair on Lag Be-Omer, thirty-two days remain. That is why we cut our hair on Lag Be-Omer and not on the thirty-fourth, for we calculate three days of Rosh Hodesh [during this period]—two days of Rosh Hodesh Iyyar and one of Rosh Hodesh Sivan. However, according to the custom which permits hair cutting after Lag Be-Omer onward, it is forbidden to cut one's hair on Rosh Hodesh Iyyar, and certainly not before that [since the result will be a drastically shortened mourning period, with a week lost at either end]. So it seems to me.

Nevertheless, [despite all this], two customs should not be observed in one city, with some inhabitants adopting one custom and others the other, because of the prohibition of forming hostile groups (לא תתגודדו).[34]

Notes

1. *Minhagei Yisrael*, pp. 101–111.
2. O.H. 493:2–3.
3. Yevamot 62a, and with variants in Kohelet Rabba 11:6, Genesis Rabba 61:3, ed. Theodor-Albeck, p. 660; the last does not mention the exact time of the deaths, but merely says that they died during one period of time (*perek ehad*).

On the customs of Sefirah, see R. Benzion Moshe Yair
Weinstock, *Siddur ha-Geonim vaha-Mequbbalim veha-Hasidim*,
vol. 11 (Jerusalem, 5737), pp. 173 f., and *Keter Shem Tov* of
R. Yom Tov Gaguine, pt. 2 (London, 5708), pp. 370–372.

4. *Meah Shearim*, p. 109.
5. His comments are cited in condensed form in Tur, O.H.
   493.
6. *Halakhot Pesuqot*, siman 97, ed. Miller (Cracow, 5653), p. 52.
   See *Otzar ha-Geonim*, Yevamot; the responsa (Jerusalem,
   5796), p. 141, sec. 327, cited in *Shaarei Teshuvah*, siman 278;
   Ha-Orah, p. 107, siman 92; *Ha-Pardes*, p. 15d, ed. Warsaw,
   siman 144 in shortened form.
7. *Netiv* 23, pt. 2, p. 147d.
8. *Otzar ha-Geonim*, Yevamot, siman 328; *Matteh Moshe*, siman
   687; Rabbenu Yeruham, Netiv 5, end of pt. 4, p. 44d; Tur,
   O.H. siman 493; see also *Shibbolei ha-Leqet*, siman 235, p.
   218; Aburdarham (Jerusalem, 5719), p. 245.
9. Tosefta Megillah 3:5, ed. Lieberman, p. 354, and parallels.
   See *Minhagei Yisrael*, vol. 4, pp. 237–238.
10. Ed. Y. Rafael (Jerusalem, 5738), vol. 2, p. 538.
    See Bekhorot 58a. Of course, fifteen days before
    Shavuot is not Lag Be-Omer, but Day 34 of the Omer; see
    below regarding our citation of Ibn Shueib. Indeed, there
    is much to discuss regarding the date of Lag Be-Omer, Day
    33 of the Omer; see below, n. 13.
    It is noteworthy that Lag Be-Omer was a fast-day in
    Eretz Israel in Byzantine times; see *Hilkhot Eretz Yisrael min
    ha-Genizah*, ed. M. Margulies (Jerusalem, 5736), p. 146,
    "Seridei Halakhah be-Siddur Eretz Yisrael": "These are the
    fasts which the Sages decreed that Israel should keep
    because of the evil events which occurred on those days:
    the eighteenth of Iyyar [= Lag Be-Omer!] Joshua son of
    Nun died." This is also noted in *Qiddush Yerahim* of R.
    Pinhas (*Hatzofeh le-Hokhmat Yisrael* 5, p. 94). It should also

be noted that Yerushalmi Taanit 3:2 (p. 66c) establishes that day for prayers for rain.

11. *Tashbetz*, vol. 1, p. 178.
12. See Meiri to Yevamot 62b.
13. See the Sermon for the First Day of Passover (Cracow, 5333), p. 41d, and see the *Beit Yosef*, O.H. 493.

In the same sermon Ibn Shueib writes: "The custom of most people not to trim their mustaches until Lag Be-Omer lacks sense." Again, he discusses the date of Lag Be-Omer. "It is not as we are accustomed [to observe], but when you subtract from forty-nine the seven days of Pass-over, the seven Sabbaths and two days of Rosh Hodesh—totaling sixteen days in which mourning should not be observed, the remainder is thirty-three, and that is the meaning of 'thirty-three days in the Omer.'" The Maharil (*Minhagim*, p. 21b) has a similar calculation, but he adds an additional day of Rosh Hodesh (two for Iyyar and one for Sivan), and so ends with thirty-two days, to which another was added as a remembrance. The difficulties with these calculations have already been noted, since the seven days of Passover include at least one Sabbath. See *Minhagei Yisrael*, vol. 4, pp. 139–141.

14. O.H. 493.
15. Vol. 2, 1/2, Hilkhot Qiddushin, siman 21, ed. Schlesinger (Berlin, 5664), p. 62.
16. Siman 235, ed. Buber, p. 218.
17. The *Beit Yosef* also writes: "There are those who are accus-tomed to have their hair cut on Rosh Hodesh Iyyar, be-cause that day is like a holiday and no mourning should be carried out on it. It seems to me that most people do not hold that custom, it is an error." R. Yosef Karo thus ruled in accordance with his opinion in the *Beit Yosef* in the Shul-han Arukh 493:3: "There are those who have their hair cut on Rosh Hodesh Iyyar, and this is an error." See also the

Minhagim of R. Isaac Tyrnau, ed. Elfenbein (New York, 5708), p. 177, n. 64, and *Minhagei R. Isaac Tyrnau*, ed. Spitzer, p. 66.

18. "I Will Remember You, My Love," and "O God, Do Not Be Silent." The first is by R. Meshullam b. Kalonimos, in Davidson's *Otzar ha-Shirah*, vol. 1, p. 109, and the second is by R. Benjamin b. R. Zerah, ibid., no. 4628.

19. Literally, "the decrees."

20. Ed. Elfenbein (New York, 5698), p. 29.

21. Ed. Dissen, p. 122 (par. 5).

22. *Sefer Maharil*, siman 21.

23. The Hebrew year 4856, corresponding to the secular year 1095/96.

24. Ed. M. Z. Weiss, *Hatzofeh le-Hokhmat Yisrael* 12 (5689): 231. According to the editor, the compiler of this work was "one of the *hasidei Italia* who lived in one of the port cities and gathered the customs of Germany and France from *sifrei minhagim* . . . after 1273."

25. See Josef Juspe Hann Neuerlingen, *Yosef Ometz*, Frankfurt-am-Main, 5688, p. 186, sect. 845. This custom is mentioned in other sources as well; see *Teshuvot u-Pesaqim me'et Hakhmei Ashkenaz ve-Tzarfat*, p. 114, siman 69, regarding the wearing of new clothes. It is clear to me that this provision is not a continuation of the words of Rav Sherira Gaon, but an addition by the compiler or his Ashkenazic source, from the end of the thirteenth century or the beginning of the fourteenth; see n. 3 there and the editor's introduction.

26. Even on the eve of Shabbat.

27. Ed. Spitzer, p. 10.

28. O.H. 284:7. See A. Epstein in the *Kaufman Festschrift*, p. 297 and Baer's Siddur, *Avodat Yisrael*, Berlin: Schocken, 5797, p. 233.

29. Jewish sources testifying to the horrors of Tatnu were collected in Haberman's important book, *Sefer Gezerot Ashke-*

naz ve-Tzarfat (Jerusalem, 5706; 2nd printing, 5731). See now R. Chazan, *European Jewry and the First Crusade* (Berkeley, 1987) and *Daggers of Faith* (Berkeley, 1993).

30. Siman 235, ed. Buber, p. 218.

31. The French custom of reciting Zidduk Hadin and Kaddish during Nisan, as noted in *Sefer ha-Minhagim deBe Maharam b.R. Barukh me-Rottenburg*, ed. Elfenbein, p. 148, may be connected with this. The whole issue needs clarification.

32. With the exception of Lag Be-Omer; see *Elya Rabba* (*Levush*, O.H. 493:4). It is not clear to me whether the prohibition of hair cutting began in Ashkenaz after Tatnu and was added to the factors which changed the preexisting mourning from geonic times, or if it was part of a development whose details I cannot yet discern. Regarding cutting the hair, see *Responsa Radvaz*, discussed in the next chapter.

   See the Taz to O.H. 493:2: "We continue some mourning [after Lag Be-Omer] because of the persecutions of Tatnu in Germany between Passover and Shavuot, as is explained in the Yotzrot and *piyyutim* we recite on those Sabbaths, which were established as *kinot* [were for Tisha Be-Av]."

33. See also Responsa Mahari Castro, *Be-Oholei Yaakov* (Livorno, 5543), siman 98. The following quotation from the Rema is from his *Darkei Moshe he-Arokh* to O.H. 493, in accordance with the Fürth פיורדא edition, 520, and is not found in the shorter edition of *Darkei Moshe*.

34. On the attitude of the Rema to custom, see Rabbi Prof. Asher Ziv, *Rabbenu Moshe Isserles (Rema)* (New York, 5732), pp. 219–261, and in particular, p. 221. On the two versions of *Darkei Moshe*, see R. Yitzhak Nissim, in his introductory article to an offset reprint of the Cracow 5338–40 edition of the Shulhan Arukh produced by Kedem Publishers (Jerusalem, 5734), n. 6. The article originally appeared in *Sinai* vol. 10 (5718): 31.

CHAPTER 9[1]
Sephardic Customs Regarding Hair-Cutting During Sefirah

THE JEWISH COMMUNITIES of France and Germany, in the wake of the persecutions and massacres which took place during the First Crusade and after, intensified their observances of the Sefirah mourning customs which had existed from geonic times, as described in the last chapter. Sephardic Jewry, on the other hand, unaffected by these events, continued the tradition of "old mourning" for the disciples of R. Akiva, but as events of the distant past, which did not call for renewal and intensification.

This may shed new light on the relations of the Sages of Sepharad to the prohibition of hair cutting during Sefirah.[2] This prohibition is rooted in custom, as R. Yosef Karo notes in the Shulhan Arukh.

It is the custom not to have one's hair cut until Lag
Be-Omer, for it is said that [the disciples of R. Akiva]
then ceased to die. . . . [In paragraph 3, the author
adds:] And some have the custom of having their
hair cut on Rosh Hodesh Iyyar, and that is an error.[3]

Now in this respect R. Yosef Karo disputes the decision of his contemporary, the Radvaz (R. David Ibn Zim-
ra, 1480–1574), who in his responsa writes the following.[4]

I myself have adopted the following practice, that
is, I have my hair cut all through Nisan and Iyyar,
and so do most people. The reason for this is that
since eulogies (*hespedim*) and fasts are prohibited
during these [= the days of Nisan], this observance
of mourning, which is [in any case] dependent on
[mere] custom, is not in force then. . . . Even for us,
who do not follow the prohibition of eulogies before Lag Be-Omer, [and should therefore be permitted to observe this mourning,] nevertheless Rosh
Hodesh Iyyar is not included [in the period of
mourning which we might have followed, but do
not], since eulogies and fasts are [certainly] prohibited then . . . and *one custom nullifies another one of no
particular force* (*minhag be-alma kol dehu*). Aside from
this, I see that many communities do not follow
this custom at all and allow hair-cutting each week
in honor of the Sabbath, according to their custom.
Since this is not a fixed observance throughout all
Israel, even though the custom of hair-cutting on
Rosh Hodesh Iyyar has no basis at all (*lo yihyeh*

minhag kelal), we follow it as the middling custom
from which we should not depart.[5]

About a century later the Italian sage R. Yaakov (b.
Shmuel) Hagiz (1620–1675) expresses himself more
sharply on this matter.[6]

> *Question:* Is it permitted to shave on the eve of the
> Sabbath before a circumcision which is to occur on
> a Sunday, which is also Lag Be-Omer?
> *Response:* . . . . [This prohibition] is an inconsequen-
> tial custom (*minhag batel be-alma*); if in the week in
> which Tisha Be-Av falls we are permitted to shave
> on the eve of the Sabbath and on Thursday, all the
> more so in regard to this *old mourning that has no
> firm source.*[7]

The Aharonim have already noted his extreme language, and the Rishon Letziyyon R. Yitzhak Nissim explained: "We must say that [he refers to] the fact that [the
custom of not shaving] is not mentioned in the Talmud.
However, they did commence the custom from that time
[= the time of the deaths of the disciples of R. Akiva]." It
seems to me that the intent of the author was that this
custom has no [real] root, not only in the Talmud, but also
not in the Geonic writings, for, as I have already shown in
the preceding chapter,[8] we find only two prohibitions in
the Geonic writings: against marrying and against per-
forming work from sunset to sunup. The prohibition of
hair-cutting comes only from the time of the Rishonim.

R. Yaakov Hagiz's younger contemporary, R. Hizkiah di Silva (1659–1698), the author of the *Pri Hadash*, follows in his spirit. In the same camp on this issue are R. Yosef Karo in Orah Hayyim 559, the Rema in Orah Hayyim 493:2 (and in his *Darkei Moshe*, ibid., n. 3), and later the *Maamar Mordekhai*,[9] *Yad Aharon*,[10] *Siddur Beit Oved* (Dinei Milah, n. 19), *Kitzur ha-Shelah*, p. 186, etc.

In the century following we have R. Yitzhak Hizkiah (b. R. Shmuel) Lampronti of Ferrara (1679–1756), in his encyclopedic *Pahad Yitzhak* (s.v. Omer, pp. 63b–64a), noting that "many are lenient in the matter of shaving each evening during Sefirah as well, [shaving] as they do all year round."[11] It seems that this statement teaches us something about the general approach regarding this prohibition in Italy.

Continuing down the generations we reach one of the greatest Sephardic Poskim since the time of R. Yosef Karo, the Hida, R. Hayyim Yosef David Azulai (1724–1800), who addresses this matter in several places. In *Responsa Hayyim Shaal*, vol. 1, siman 6, for example, he writes:

> Whoever examines this matter carefully and investigates the roots of the issue will come to the clear and certain conclusion that *this is a very inconsequential custom.* . . . You will realize how inconsequential it is, *and it may be cast aside for any reason.* . . . Again I say that this custom has no foundation or sufficient reason. . . . According to the plain meaning, we have no firm and sufficient reason to forbid shaving.

In his *Yosef Ometz*, he quotes R. Yaakov (b. Avraham) Castro (1525–1610), the Maharikas, who declares that when refraining from shaving is uncomfortable there is reason to be lenient, and expresses himself in similar terms to the Radvaz's responsum quoted above. "This custom is not preferable to the positive mitzvah of sukkah, regarding which the rule is that one who suffers from the performance of the mitzvah is relieved of it. Certainly a person may suffer greater inconvenience in thirty-three days!"[12]

The contrast between this attitude and that of Ashkenazic Poskim is striking. The Ashkenazic R. Yosef b. R. Moshe (1423–1490?) reports that his teacher, the author of *Terumat ha-Deshen*, R. Yisrael b. Petahiah Ashkenazi Isserlin of Austria (1390–1460),

> did not wish to permit the *baal berit*, who is called a *kvatter*, or the mohel to shave on 3 Iyyar. My teacher R. Yosef Kolon, may God guard him, [while] permitted in Mestre[13] a *baal berit* to shave on 6 Iyyar, but my teacher R. Yudah Overnik [a disciple of the *Terumat ha-Deshen* and teacher of the author of the *Leqet Yosher*, who died in 1510] said that the two cases are not similar, for the one who shaved appeared only after the circumcision and there was great wonder, for it was not known that he had been at a circumcision during the Omer.[14]

We see the difference between the approach of the Italian sage R. Y. Kolon, whose was of French origin but

is lenient in the matter of shaving during Sefirah, and
that of the contemporary Sages of Ashkenaz, who were
strict.

This quotation seems to reflect accurately the differing approaches of the two groups.[15] The lenient approach of the Sephardic Poskim is tied to the fact that
this "inconsequential" custom reflects an *old* mourning
for the deaths of the disciples of R. Akiva. In contrast,
the Ashkenazic Poskim felt, in the words of *Sefer Minhag
Tov*, siman 61,

> It is a proper custom not to have one's hair cut, and
> not to put on new clothing or any new thing, or to
> luxuriate in a bathhouse, to cut one's nails after
> Passover till Shavuot, in honor of the pure and right-
> eous pious ones who sacrificed themselves for the
> sanctification of God's Name. But on Lag Be-Omer it
> is permitted to do all these, because of the miracle
> which occurred then. [However,] from Lag Be-Omer
> till Shavuot the prohibition remains in force.[16]

It seems that the farther from Ashkenaz we are, the
more lenient the attitude becomes. This may be illustrat-
ed by the words of the *Sefer Shoshanat ha-Melekh*, by the
Yemenite R. Shalom bin Yahya Habshush, whose book is
a condensation of *Responsa Peulat Zaddik* by R. Yahya
Salah, who passed away in 5565 (1805).

> The ancient custom is to shave on the eve of the
> Sabbath during Sefirah in honor of the Sabbath, for

the positive mitzvah of a prophet is preferable to a custom, and it is written, "and you shall call the Sabbath a pleasure." About forty years ago a sage came from the islands and forced the community against its will [to accept the custom] of not shaving, with the help of the Leader Rashba, and according to the decision of R. R. Mashriki,[17] for his own reasons, but now we are returning to the old custom, for we have seen how concerned Hazal were not to cause discomfort on Shabbat. Indeed, even during the Sabbaths of Sefirah, they warned not to recite *kinot* or mourn over Jerusalem. It is all the more certain that showing signs of mourning on Shabbat regarding something which is not even an obligation during the week [is forbidden] all the more on Shabbat! For when we see a person's hair grow long in mourning, causing him discomfort so that he has to scratch his head because of the sweat and heat[18]—there is no greater nullification of the "pleasure of Shabbat" than that!

And even though there are still those in the city who hold to the custom of not shaving, this is not a violation of the prohibition of setting up separate groups with differing customs (*lo titgodedu*), for this applies only with respect to something whose origin is in Torah law, not to matters which are not essential. Moreover, each community is considered to be its own court, and when two courts reach different decisions it is not a violation of *lo titgodedu*.[19]

Indeed, even those who are accustomed not to shave may return to the old custom without the need to have their oath nullified (*be-lo petah uve-lo haratah*), even though they themselves and their fathers have followed the custom of not shaving for many years, since, after all, they were forced to do so against their will. And even if they accepted the [new, strict custom] willingly, it was an erroneous acceptance, for they thought that the prohibition was an actual [halakhic one, and not merely a custom]. Even more so, even if they accepted the custom willingly as a fence and for greater piety, their new custom may be nullified with the due expression of regret before a court (*petah ve-haratah*). Indeed, even individuals may ask for their custom to be nullified, even if the whole community does not do so.[20]

Only one far removed from the communities of Ashkenaz could write in this vein.

Notes

1. *Minhagei Yisrael*, pp. 112–117.
2. This issue has been discussed by many of the greatest of the Aharonim; see the responsum of R. Yitzhak Nissim, in the collection of R. Nahum Rackover, *Hilkhot Yom ha-Atzma'ut ve-Yom Yerushalayim* (Jerusalem, 5745), pp. 334–340, as well as the responsum of R. Ovadiah Haddaya (pp. 331–333). Also, see the material gathered by R. Zvi Kohen in *Bein Pesah li-Shevuot*, chap. 9, pp. 238 f., and Y. Gilat, *Bar-Ilan* 18-19 (5741): 89.
3. O.H. 493:2–3. See the comments of the *Maamar Mordekhai*, R. Mordekhai Karmi Carpenteras (Livorno, 5538) to O.H. 493:7, and also the *Peri Hadash* to 493:3, citing the Maha-

ram Lonzano, to the effect that this is a proper custom. But there are conflicting views; see below, and see the addendum to chap. 8 and n. 17 to the same chapter.

4. Vol. 2, no. 697.

5. It is interesting to note that the Radvaz's decision was still followed in Egypt as late as the nineteenth century; see *Nehar Mitzrayim* of R. Rafael Aharon Ibn Shimon (Memphis, 5668), p. 33a, n. 27, who cites R. Yom Tov b. R. Eliyahu Yisrael in his *Sefer Minhagei Mitzrayim: Minhagei ha-Ir Cairo* (Jerusalem, 5633). Even though R. Ibn Shimon wanted to change the existing practice, his responsum informs us of the lenient practice.

6. In his *Halakhot Qetanot*, siman 33.

7. Literally, "root."

8. See above, chap. 9, n. 17.

9. Even expanding the range of those connected with the circumcision celebration who may shave to include the father, the sandek, and the mohel.

10. Of R. Aharon Alfandari (Izmir, 5495).

11. See the words of the Radvaz above.

12. *Oholei Yaakov*, siman 98. And see what is written about the Maharikas in *Yosef Ometz*: "the halakhot of his teacher the Radvaz, z.l., are in his mouth."

13. R. Yosef Kolon (1420?–1480) was in Mestre till before 1467, and it was there that the author of *Leqet Yosher*, who studied with Mahari Weil and Mahari Minz, also studied with him.

14. *Leqet Yosher*, Heleq O.H. (Berlin, 5663), p. 97.

15. The situation is not different in regard to marriage during Sefirah; see the responsum of R. Nissim cited above, pp. 335, 339, for the Radvaz, Maharam Lonzano, and the *Pri Hadash* all permitted marriage for one who had not yet fulfilled the mitzvah of having children; a similar custom was in effect in Jerusalem and various other communities.

However, the view of the Arizal and his disciples was that one should not shave on Rosh Hodesh Iyyar or on Lag Be-Omer under any circumstances, for a great kabbalistic reason. See A. Yaari, *Tarbiz* 31 (5722): 90, 92.

16. Ed. M. Z. Weiss, *Hatzofeh le-Hokhmat Yisrael* 12 (5689): 231. See above, chap. 8, n. 24.

17. See the introduction to *Shoshanat ha-Melekh* on this personage.

18. On this, see R. Sh. Z. Braun, *Shearim Metzuyyanim ba-Halakhah*, vol. 3 (Jerusalem–New York, 5738), p. 124, and in *Responsa Yehavveh Daat* of R. Ovadiah Yosef, vol. 1 (Jerusalem, 5737), siman 38, regarding washing during the Three Weeks, and the factor of heat and sweat in southern lands. See also *Responsa Hatam Sofer*, Y.D. 348; *Noda Bi-Yehudah*, mahadura qamma, siman 14; and Maharam Schick on Y.D. 371. On the influence of climatic conditions on the halakha, see *Minhagei Yisrael*, vol. 3 (1994), pp. 70 *et seq.*

19. On the principle of *lo titgodedu*, see *Minhagei Yisrael*, vol. 3, pp. 108–111.

20. *Shoshanat ha-Melekh*, ed. R. Shimon Gridi (Jerusalem, 5727), pp. 35a–b (Dinei Sefirat ha-Omer, siman 5). My thanks to my student Mr. Saadiah Madmon, who brought this source to my attention.

PART V
SHAVUOT

CHAPTER 10[1]
Spreading Grasses in Synagogues on Shavuot

THE CUSTOM OF "spreading grasses on Shavuot in synagogues and homes as a remembrance of Mattan Torah"
is well known (Rema, O.H. 494:3).[2] Many reasons have
been given for this custom, and there was even a debate
over it, as we shall see. The *Levush* and *Birkei Yosef* (to
O.H.) wrote that the custom is a remembrance of Mattan
Torah, when grass covered Mount Sinai, as is written,
"The sheep and cattle should not pasture [at the foot of
the mountain]."[3] This indicates that there was pasturage
there.[4]

A midrashic comment is reported, based on the Biblical text "your lips are roses,"[5] to the effect that "at every utterance which issued from the mouth of the Holy One, blessed be He, the world was filled with spices."[6]

However, the Magen Avraham gives a different reason entirely: "because on Shavuot we are judged regarding the fruit of trees [and so plants are spread out in synagogues to remind us] to pray for them."[7]

In the *Benei Yissaskhar*, by the Hasidic rebbe, R. Zvi Elimelekh Shapira, there is another explanation, based on Midrash Leviticus Rabba 23:3, wherein Israel is compared to a rose, and the world to an orchard. The King wishes to destroy the orchard, but refrains from doing so when He sees the rose, and in its merit saves the world. So too Israel, which received the Torah, is compared to a rose which saves the orchard (= the world).[8]

The custom, apparently of Ashkenazic origin, to set up trees and flowers around the holy ark, walls, and doors of the synagogue, was a source of great concern to the Vilna Gaon, who tried to stamp it out of existence "because it is now a gentile custom to set up trees on their holiday."[9] However, the author of *Orhot Hayyim he-Hadash* wrote in defense of the custom that "everything which is done for a reason cannot be considered forbidden as a gentile custom."[10]

Yet another reason given for this custom connects it with the bringing of first fruits to the Temple, a mitzvah whose time was Shavuot. However, none of these reasons fully satisfies us. It is possible that there is yet another reason, different from the ones given, while the custom developed and changed its form within the matrix of reasons which arose after the fact. Perhaps the most convincing reason of all is the one that connects it with Shavuot as the day on which we are judged in regard to the fruit of trees.

However, I have yet another reason to suggest, though tentatively. In 1940 the scholar Jacob Mann published a previously unknown midrash on the Torah.[11] In a piece devoted to Exodus 19:11 on the verse "Be prepared for the third day," the midrash says:

> Why the third day? For on the third day [of Creation] the trees and grasses were created, as it is written, "God said: Let the earth flower forth" (Genesis 1:11). On the third day I created the necessities of life, and the Torah too is called "the tree of life," as it is written, "It is a tree of life for those who seize hold of it" (Proverbs 3:18). And I gave it over [to Israel] on the third day, as it is written, "For on the third day [God will descend onto Mount Sinai in sight of all Israel]" (Exodus 19:11).

The verbal association—a sort of *gezerah shavah*—between the third day of Creation, when trees and grasses were created, and the third day when the Holy One, blessed be He, descended onto Mount Sinai and gave us the Torah, serves as the basis for this midrash. It could easily have occurred to the medieval Sages who established the custom. Thus the custom of spreading grass and setting up trees in synagogues may have arisen and developed out of this associative thinking.

Even if this is not the essential origin of our custom, it could easily have served as a subsidiary reason. However, since I have yet to find this reason given in the sources, the issue remains speculative.

Notes

1. *Minhagei Yisrael*, pp. 118–120.
2. Following the Maharil, *Minhagim*, Hilkhot Shavuot. A similar custom exists in Egypt, according to R. Neveh Shalom, R. Eliyahu Hazzan, *Minhagei Na Amon u-Mitzrayim* (5654), siman 494, cited in *Keter Shem Tov* of R. Yom Tov Gaguine, pts. 4–5, Shavuot, 1954, p. 13, except there the same custom existed for Simhat Torah. In Persia Shavuot is also known as "the holiday of flowers."
3. Exodus 34:3.
4. See the picture from an Ashkenazic *mahzor* of the fourteenth century in I. Abrahams, *Jewish Life in the Middle Ages* (New York, 1982), p. 267.
5. Song of Songs 5:13.
6. Reported by R. Gaguine (see above, n. 2) in the name of *Sefer Atiq Yomin*.
7. This is based on Mishnah Rosh Hashanah 1:2; on Shavuot we are judged in regard to the fruit of trees. See Zohar II, 96a. This custom has no relation to a similar one in regard to Yom Kippur; there the reason is to cover the floors so that those who prostrate themselves will not touch the floor directly with their heads and knees; see R. Yosef Finkelstein, *Meqorei ha-Dinim* (Warsaw, 5634).
8. (Zolkiew-Lvov, 5606), Hodesh Sivan, maamar 4, n. 7.
9. Cited in *Mishnah Berurah* to O.H. 494, n. 10. See also R. Hayyim Elazar Shapira, *Shaar Yisaskhar* (Munkatch, 5698),

Maamar Hag ha-Bikkurim, n. 48, and R. Avraham b. R. Yehiel Mikhel Danzig, *Hayyei Adam* (Vilna, 5570), kelal 131, n. 13.
10. Siman 494, n. 8. He cites, among other sources, *Responsa Rivash*, siman 158. See also my comments in *Minhagei Yisrael*, vol. 4, p. 30.
11. Jacob Mann, *The Bible as Read and Preached in the Old Synagogue*, vol. 1 (Cincinnati, 1940), vol. 2 (New York, 1971).

PART VI
THE THREE WEEKS

CHAPTER 11[1]
The Dispute Over Announcing a Fast

R. YOSEF KARO WRITES in his Shulhan Arukh, O.H. 550:4: "On the Sabbath before a fast the *sheliah tzibbur* announces the fast, with the exception of Tisha Be-Av and the fast of Yom Kippur and the fast of Esther.[2] The mnemonic is **A**[v]-**K**[ippur]-**P**[urim]—*akaf alav pihu*.[3] In his note there the Rema writes: "[However,] the custom of [us] Ashkenazim is not to announce any one of them,"[4] and the *Levush* records the same fact. Ashkenazim and Sephardim thus differ on this point.[5]

Three points must be clarified: (1) the origin of this custom; (2) why it was not accepted by Ashkenazic communities; (3) why Yom Kippur, Tisha Be-Av, and Taanit Purim are excluded from the "announcement."

First, let us examine the source of R. Yosef Karo's formulation. In the *Beit Yosef*, R. Karo cites the Aburdarham as the source for the custom.

> On the Sabbath preceding them [= the fasts], after the Haftarah and before Ashre, it is necessary for the *sheliah tzibbur* to announce and let the congregation know on which day the fast will fall. He says: "Fellow Israelites, listen! Such-and-such a fast will fall on such-and-such a day; may God turn it to joy and rejoicing, as He promised us in [His] consolatory [prophecies], and let us say: Amen." [However,] three fasts are not announced: Tisha Be-Av, Yom Kippur, and Purim; the mnemonic is *Akaf*.

Mahzor Vitry gives a bit more detail: After the Mi She-asah part of the Kiddush Hahodesh, the *sheliah tzibbur* says as follows:

> Such-and-such a fast on such-and-such a day which is coming upon us, may God turn it for us and all Israel to joy and rejoicing, blessing and peace, as is written: "So says God: The fast of the fourth [month], the fast of the fifth [month], the fast of the seventh [month], the fast of the tenth [month] will be transformed to joy and rejoicing for the House of Judah, for happy[6] appointed times; truth and peace do they love" (Zechariah 8:19).

As to the reason for this custom, it would seem that it may be found in O.H. 562:12,[7] where R. Karo rules that individuals need not accept a communal fast day on their own, but rather the *sheliah tzibbur* announces it, "and it is [as though] accepted."[8] In condensing the words of the Tur, R. Karo omitted the following clause: "all the more so in the case of fasts which have a Biblical basis." From this, it would seem that even such fasts need to be announced, and individuals need not accept them at Minhah time.

The *Levush* on O.H. 562 disagrees, however, and holds that individuals *cannot* accept the fasts themselves, for they are sworn to observe them from Biblical times. The same applies to fasts which the community accepts on itself; again the individual has no choice in the matter, and individual acceptance is not necessary or possible. The *sheliah tzibbur*, by his announcement, accepts the fast for all, by authority of the Bet Din.[9] It would seem that the Ashkenazic custom is based on these considerations.

Now that we understand the reasons for the Ashkenazic approach to the question of announcing the fast, it is all the more difficult to understand R. Yosef Karo's approach. In order to understand it we must look closely at the mention of the verse from Zechariah in the formulation of the announcement in *Mahzor Vitry*. This verse is expounded at length in a well-known sugya in Rosh Hashanah 18a.

What [is the meaning of] that which is written: "So says the Lord of Hosts: 'The fast of the fourth

[month], the fast of the fifth [month], the fast of the
seventh [month], the fast of the tenth [month] will
be transformed to joy and rejoicing [for the House of
Judah, for happy appointed times; truth and peace
do they love]"? He calls them "fasts" and calls them
"[times of] joy and rejoicing"! [The answer is:] At
times of peace they will be [times of] joy and rejoicing; if there is no peace, [there will be] fasts.

Said R. Papa: This is what it means to say: At
times of peace they will be [times of] joy and rejoicing. If there is persecution,[10] there is a fast; if there
is no persecution, if they wish they may fast; if they
wish they may not fast.

If so, should this apply to Tisha Be-Av also?

Said R. Papa:[11] Tisha Be-Av is different, because
troubles multiplied on that day.

From this sugya we see that the obligation to retain
these fasts—aside from Tisha Be-Av—in our own time, a
time when there is no peace but also no active persecution, depends on whether the community wishes it or
not.

This is the rule on which a number of Geonim and
Rishonim decided. As an example, see the opinion of the
Gaon cited in *Shibbolei ha-Leqet*, siman 2778:[12] "As to the
four fasts, Mar Rav Kohen Tzedek Gaon wrote: Whoever wishes to fast may fast, and whoever wishes not to
fast need not fast, except for Tisha Be-Av."

A similar Geonic decision is recorded in a responsum published in *Ginzei Qedem*, vol. 3:[13]

As to that which you asked regarding the four fasts, whether they have been abolished. . . . Therefore, there is no objection to whoever wishes not to fast on the three fasts; there is no obligation. But Tisha Be-Av [is different]; since [troubles] multiplied on that day, one is obligated to fast and treat it as Yom Kippur, for so did the Sages say:[14] "Rava expounded: 'Pregnant and nursing women must complete the fast in the same manner as Yom Kippur, and [everything forbidden on that day is likewise] forbidden at twilight.'"[15]

This is also the opinion of Rabbenu Hananel: "[If] there is no persecution and no peace, *as at the present time*, if they wish to, they may fast; if they wish not to, they may not fast."[16] Many others hold this opinion: *Sefer ha-Eshkol*, in the name of a Gaon; the Rashba in his *hiddushim* there; the Ran; the *Nimmukei Yosef* to Rosh Hashanah as well as to the Rif there.

However, the Ramban does not. In his *Torat ha-Adam*, Inyan Avelut Yeshana,[17] he writes:

Now they have already accepted [these fasts], and therefore it is forbidden for an individual to depart from the ways of the community—all the more so in these generations, for because of our sins troubles have multiplied in Israel and there is no peace. Therefore all are obligated to fast *by tradition and by the enactment of the Prophets*.[18]

This is the decision of the Tur in O.H. 550.

> Now they [= the community] have wished it, and
> the custom is to fast. Therefore it is forbidden to
> depart from this, all the more so in our generations.
> Therefore all are obligated to fast *by tradition and by
> the enactment of the Prophets.*

Thus the Tur accepts the formulation of the Ramban.
So too, the Shulhan Arukh, except that there are minor
changes in the formulation by the omission of several
words—"by tradition and by the enactment of the
Prophets." This omission may imply that the reason for
the fast is communal acceptance and not an old tradition.

The sources we have cited indicate that there is a
profound disagreement in regard to the obligation of
observing these three fasts. According to one opinion,
the obligation is based on the wishes of each individual;
according to the other, the fasts are obligatory for every
Jew, irrespective of his or her wishes.

Nevertheless it is necessary to stress, that even
according to those who hold that fasting is an individual
decision, the fact remains that now "they are accustomed to fast." Thus there is an obligation on the individual not to depart from the ways of the community
and therefore to follow this custom and observe the
fasts. However, since ultimately, the decision is the individual's, according to this view, the custom of announcing the forthcoming fast was enacted, so as to serve as a
medium for individual acceptance. And that is precisely
what the Shulhan Arukh records, by authority of the
Abudarham.

On the other hand, those who see the fasts as being observed *by tradition and by the enactment of the Prophets*, view the "announcement" as implying disrespect to this hoary tradition and to the authority of the Prophets.

Now we can answer the third question we posed at the head of this chapter: What is the reason for the difference between the three fasts of Tisha Be-Av, Yom Kippur, and Taanit Esther and the others? There is no question as to Yom Kippur, of course, which is obligatory from Sinai; and, as we have seen, no one has ever doubted the obligatory nature of Tisha Be-Av, because "troubles multiplied on it."

As to Taanit Esther, this fast is not announced because it is *not* obligatory, as the Rema notes in Shulhan Arukh, O.H. 684:2, and so it is not announced as though it were obligatory.

Thus, two of the fasts are not announced precisely because of their universal applicability, and the third, Taanit Esther, is not announced because it lacks such applicability.[19]

Notes

1. *Minhagei Yisrael*, pp. 169–177.
2. The way R. Karo refers to the fast of Esther as the "fast of Purim" is noteworthy. This usage may have been dictated by the title of this siman in the Shulhan Arukh which includes the word *tzom* to some extent, though it appears earlier, in the *Sefer Mitzvot Zemaniyot* of R. Yisrael b.R. Yosef ha-Yisraeli of Toledo, ed. Blau (New York, 5744).
3. Job 16:26.
4. He writes similarly in his *Darkei Moshe* there.

5. Some Sephardic communities follow the same custom as that of Ashkenazim; see *Nehar Mitzrayim* of R. Refael Aharon ibn Shimon, Hilkhot Taanit, siman 1 (38b–39b), who cites the earlier *Sefer Minhagei Mitzrayim: Minhagei ha-Ir Cairo* of R. Yom Tov b. R. Eliyahu Yisrael (Jerusalem, 5633), siman 57, though he himself protests against this practice, since, to his mind, the announcement is intended to ensure that the fast is observed.

6. Literally: "Good."

7. This is pointed out in *Kaf ha-Hayyim* 550:25, who cites *Sefer Yafeh le-Lev* of R. Rahamim Yitzhak Palaggi, pt. 2, no. 4. Note, however, that *Kaf ha-Hayyim* cites a different part of the same work (pt. 3, no. 4) in the next paragraph (550:26), where a different reason is given: to make the community aware of the fast.

8. See further on where he notes: "Some say that this refers only to the land of Israel, which had a patriarch [ruling over it], but outside the land of Israel everyone must accept the fast individually." For the sources of this rule, see *Beit Yosef*.

9. *Eliyahu Zuta* holds the same view; see ibid., n. 11, and see further in *Kaf ha-Hayyim* 562, n. 73.

10. Literally, "A decree of the kingdom." See *Dikdukei Soferim* there, p. 40, n. *vav*; the reading of MS Munich is, "If there is no peace and there is persecution—fast; [if there is] no peace and no persecution . . ." See the notes there, and compare the version of the *Halakhot Gedolot*, ed. Hildesheimer (grandson), p. 390.

11. See *Dikdukei Soferim* there; in addition, a marginal note records the reading of the Tur, O.H. 550: "Rava."

12. Ed. Buber, p. 263, cited in *Otzar ha-Geonim* to Rosh Hashanah, p. 33.

13. (Haifa, 1925), pp. 42–43.

14. Pesahim 54b.

15. Cited in *Otzar ha-Geonim* there, p. 32.

16. Rabbenu Hananel to Rosh Hashanah 18a.

17. Ed. Chavel in *Kitvei ha-Ramban*, vol. 2, p. 243.

18. His opinion is cited in *Orhot Hayyim* and in the Ran there. As noted above, the Rashba disagrees, and disputes the Ramban's view in his comments. However, the *Eshkol* follows the same view as the Ramban, as does R. Ephraim b. R. Yaakov of Bonn (a disciple of R. Shmuel b. Natronai, the son-in-law of the Raavan), as we see from a manuscript of his commentaries (MS Hamburg 152), p. 147e: "Our ancestors have accepted these Scriptural fasts, in the wake of the many persecutions, as set communal fasts." This is cited in R. Avraham b. R. Azriel, *Arugat ha-Bosem*, ed. Urbach, vol. 4 (Jerusalem, 1963), p. 42.

19. See, for example, "Hagahot ha-Minhagim" in R. Isaac Tyrnau's *Sefer ha-Minhagim*, p. 154: "The reason is that this fast has no support from any place, though Rabbenu Tam found some hint of it in Megillah 2a, where it states that 13 Adar is 'the time of the community for all'." Rabbenu Tam's view is cited by the Rosh, Megillah, chap. 1, siman 1, and in the *Mordekhai* there, siman 776.

    Indeed, Rabbenu Tam's reasoning is to be found much earlier, in the *She'iltot*, Vayakhel, siman 66, ed. Mirsky, vol. 3 (Jerusalem, 5724), siman 79, a *she'ilta* known to the *Kaftor va-Ferah*, 39, ed. Edelman, p. 87b, and to the *Or Zarua*, vol. 2, siman 367, and to other Rishonim. Thus, the source of Taanit Esther is to be found, at the very latest, in the *earliest* post-Talmudic work, where it is connected with Megillah 2a.

    Despite all this, the connection is vague enough to warrant the judgment of many Rishonim and Aharonim that the fast has little support in the sources, even though it may be mentioned, and that its real authority is one of custom; see the *Agudah* of R. Alexander Zuslein to Megillah, siman 1 (Jerusalem, 5726), p. 81; *Sefer Minhagim* of R. Avraham Klausner, ed. Disin, p. 75, siman 81, sec. 3; *Mahzor Vitry*, siman 245, p. 210; *Sefer ha-Pardes* of Rashi, siman 204, ed. Ehrenreich (Budapest, 5684), p. 252; *Shibbolei ha-Leqet* siman 194, ed. Buber, p. 76; *Orhot Hayyim*, Hilkhot Megillah u-Purim, siman 26 (Jerusalem, 5716), p. 267—and already in the Meiri, *Magen Avot*, siman 23, and even the Rambam, Hilkhot Taanit 5:5. See also my grandfather's ל״צז responsa, *Afarqasta de-Anya*, vol. 1, 2nd ed. (Jerusalem, 5741), siman 188, p. 158a.

Indeed, the extent to which the fast has no real support in the sources can be gauged by the *Levush*'s attempt to ground it in those sources; see O.H. 686:2. "The [Jews] accepted upon themselves an obligatory communal fast [on 13 Adar] because on that day they gathered in the days of Mordecai and Esther to fight and defend themselves. They must have had to beseech compassion [from God] and [say] Selihot and Tahanunim, and *presumably* they fasted on that day, for we find in a midrash that Moshe Rabbenu fasted on the day he fought Amalek, and so they *certainly must have fasted* on the day they fought with their enemies in the time of Mordecai and Esther. And since we observe the days of Purim as a memorial for that miracle, we must also observe the fast, the Selihot, and Tahanunim as they did."

It is worth noting that this fast is called "Taanit Esther" not because of the fast Esther herself fasted, but because of the "days of fasts and prayer" mentioned in Esther 9:31—the fast that Esther proclaimed. There is, however, another fast day recorded in Soferim 17:3, ed. Higger (New York, 5697), p. 299, which was observed in memory of Esther's own fast: "The three days of [Esther's] fast are observed not consecutively but spaced out: Monday-Thursday-Monday. Our teachers in Eretz Israel are accustomed to fasting these days after Purim, because of [the days of] Nicanor and other [days on which it used to be forbidden to fast], and, furthermore, we delay negative observances [when necessary]; we do not observe them earlier than need be." Another reason for not fasting during Nisan is given in Soferim 21:1—the celebrations accompanying the inauguration of the Tabernacle were held during the first twelve days of the month. This observance of the three-day fast is mentioned in Shulhan Arukh, O.H. 686:3, though its non-obligatory nature is stressed. See above, chap. 6.

Thus there are two different fasts associated with Purim. In Eretz Israel they observed a three-day fast after Purim and not in Nisan, and the one-day fast was observed as "the day of congregation" in Babylon, apparently, and which is mentioned in She'iltot and perhaps in the Bavli.

However, in an article I published in 1986, in the *Journal for the Study of Judaism* 16, I suggested that the way in which this day is mentioned in the *She'iltot*, in the name of R. Shmuel b. Yitzhak, a Babylonian Amoral who emigrated to Eretz Israel, "as R. Shmuel b. Yitzhak said . . . ," indicates that he originally made this remark in another connection, from where it was quoted in Megillah. It may be that originally his comment was made in connection with this fast, but was then cited in Megillah as proof for the reading of the Megillah on 13 Adar. If this is true, the fast may have been observed as far back as the third century, at least in Babylon. See the comments of Y. Tabory, *Tarbiz* 55 (1986): 264.

CHAPTER 12[1]
The Prohibition of Eating Meat and Drinking Wine During the Three Weeks

THE WORDS OF THE Shulhan Arukh, Orah Hayyim 551:9, are well known: "It is customary not to eat meat or drink wine during this week [= the week during which Tisha Be-Av falls]. . . . Some add [the days] from Rosh Hodesh [Av], and some add [still more], from 17 Tammuz."

It is beyond doubt that these prohibitions were not observed in the time of the Tannaim or the Amoraim, for in the long sugya at the end of Taanit the prohibition of eating meat or drinking wine is limited to the last meal before the fast of Tisha Be-Av, according to R. Meir, while the Sages merely require that consumption of these foods be *limited*, not prohibited—and only during that meal! Thus, according to the majority opinion, one is permitted to eat meat and drink wine even immediately before Tisha Be-Av.

If so, the question arises: Where does this custom come from?

Its source seems to be a quotation from the Yerushalmi cited by several Rishonim. In *Sefer ha-Manhig*, ed. Rafael (Jerusalem, 5738), p. 297, we read:

> R. Hai Gaon wrote: "Even though it is said in Yerushalmi Taanit and Pesahim:[2] R. Zeira said: Women who are accustomed not to drink wine and not to eat meat[3] from [the time] that Av arrives until the end of the fast, [it is] a custom, for then the Even Shetiyah [= the Foundation Stone, upon which the world was created, and which was located in the Temple][4] ceased."

Mahzor Vitry, siman 263, p. 225, cites the same source with some slight variations:

> Our women do not drink wine from 17 Tammuz until 9 Av—it is a custom. And most Geonim were accustomed not to eat meat or drink wine from the beginning of Av till [after] 9 Av . . . and some begin earlier—from 17 Tammuz to 9 Av.[5]

There are even cases where two versions of the Yerushalmi are cited in one work, as though they were two separate sources. Thus, the *Kol Bo*, Hilkhot Tisha Be-Av, has the following: "Yerushalmi: Said R. Ze'ira: Women who are accustomed not to drink wine from when Av arrives—it is a custom." And in the same work, at the end of Hilkhot Tisha Be-Av: "Yerushalmi: Our women who do not drink wine from 17 Tammuz to 9 Av—it is a custom."

R. Saul Lieberman already noted that these are not the original versions of the Yerushalmi, for the Geonim and Rishonim cite yet another version. See, for example, *Or Zarua*, volume 2, siman 414, p. 84a:

> From when Av arrives we diminish our rejoicing, and people have already been accustomed not to eat meat or drink wine . . . from when Av arrives. There is a support for this custom, for we say in the first chapter of our tractate (Taanit 6:1) in the Yerushalmi: Said R. Zeira: "Women who are accustomed not to drink wine from when Av arrives—it is a custom, for then the Shetiyah ceased.

However, Rav Nissim Gaon[6] did not have the reading "'wine' (חמר) but to spin 'wool' (עמרא), and its meaning is related to שתי או ערב, 'weft and woof,' but he does not speak about drinking wine at all." Indeed, our printed Yerushalmi (Venice edition) in Pesahim and Taanit has: "Women who are accustomed not to למשתייא from when Av arrives—it is a custom, for then the Shetiyah Stone ceased. What is the reason? 'For the foundations are destroyed' (Psalms 11:3)."[7]

R. S. Lieberman wrote that "the printed version is the correct one without doubt, and its interpretation is as Rav Nissim Gaon suggested, למשתי = to spin, to weave. And the other versions are additions and interpretations."[8] Indeed, it is customary for women to spin wool, and the Foundation Stone is that from which the world was founded and spun. And if the subject of this Yerushalmi was to refrain from eating meat and drinking wine, why should it be limited to women alone? And what is the connection with the cessation of the Foundation Stone?[9]

Thus, the original reading of the Yerushalmi was: "Women who are accustomed to spin," and in ancient times the word "wool" was added to explain the reference more clearly. However, the Western Aramaic word עמר was changed at some point for חמר or חמרא, which could be (and was) interpreted as "wine." We find the following version in the Auerbach edition of the *Eshkol*, עמרא דלא למשתא,[10] but in the Albeck edition we have: דלא למשתא חמרא! And this חמרא was interpreted as "wine." From the spelling חמר R. Lieberman learned that this addition was made in Eretz Israel, since the Babylonians would have spelled the word with an *alef* at the end, חמרא. From this we see the accuracy of *Or Zarua* and *Magen Avot*.[11]

The discussion of these variants brings to mind the words of the Babylonian Talmud Eruvin 53b: "The inhabitants of Judah were precise in their language . . . [but] the inhabitants of the Galilee were not precise," after which a story is told of a Galilean who said, אמר למאן אמר למאן. "They said to him: 'Foolish Galilean!

חמר [a donkey] to ride or חמר [wine] to drink? עמר [wool] to wear or אימר [a sheep = a fleece] to cover oneself?'" From this story we learn that the Galileans did not distinguish between the words for "wine" and "donkey," and for "wool" and "sheep," precisely because they could not distinguish the letters *het* and *ayin*.[12] There are many such examples, as when R. Berekhiah quotes R. Levi in Genesis Rabba 63:5, p. 681, as glossing the verse "Isaac prayed" (ויעתר)[13] by means of the word חותר, "to beseech." Or the interchange of the words תוחלת and תועלת. Thus it is not surprising that חמר and עמר should be interchanged. However, in the course of time the Eretz Israel form חמר was understood as "wine" under the influence of those familiar with the Aramaic of the Babylonian Talmud. Once "wool" was converted to "wine," the addition of "meat" by scribes was almost inevitable.[14]

We conclude, therefore, that the pronunciation of the early Eretz Israel spelling of עמר-חמר, and the lack of understanding of this by later scribes in Babylon (?) in the time of the Geonim created[15] the custom of refraining from eating meat and drinking wine in the period between 17 Tammuz and 9 Av—"*Bein ha-Metzarim.*"[16]

There is yet another source in which the custom of refraining from meat and wine during the Three Weeks is referred to—Daniel 10:2–3, where Daniel reports that "in those days, I, Daniel, mourned three full weeks.[17] I ate no tasty bread I did not eat, and meat and wine did not come to my mouth; I did not anoint myself at all until three weeks were complete." These verses in Daniel served as a sort of explicit source for this custom, as the Tur explains in O.H. 551.

There are pious people who fast from 17 Tammuz onward. Others refrain from meat and wine. And we learn in the Yerushalmi: How long is it between 17 Tammuz and 9 Av? Twenty-one days, from the time that the city was broken into until the Temple was destroyed. *Others say: [This] corresponds to the three weeks which Daniel fasted.* [But] the custom of Ashkenaz is for individuals to refrain from meat and wine from 17 Tammuz onward.

The *Beit Yosef* comments on this: "Others say: '[This] corresponds to the three weeks which Daniel fasted'— this too is there in the name of Rabbenu Saadiah." *Beit Yosef*'s reference is apparently to *Hagahot Maimuniyot,* which is referred to earlier in *Beit Yosef* to *Mishneh Torah,* Hilkhot Taanit 5:6; I have not found that reference there. However, I found that tradition in *Tanya Rabbati,* p. 126, as follows:

I found in the name of R. Saadiah Gaon ז״ל that from 17 Tammuz till 9 Av are the days mentioned in Daniel during which Daniel fasted three weeks. Some are careful not to eat meat and drink wine, as is written, "and meat and wine did not come to my mouth." [However,] others say that this refers to the month of Nisan.

It seems that the R. Saadiah Gaon here is not the one we
usually think of, the Egyptian, but rather one who lived
in France. The noted historian of French Jewry, Samuel
Poznanski, touches on this in an article devoted to the
more famous R. Saadiah.[18]

> As far as I know, the one who first realized that
> there was someone named Saadiah in France was
> [S.Y.] Rapaport, who relied on the following read-
> ing in *Liqqutei ha-Pardes*, published in Amsterdam,
> p. 17b: "R. Saadiah told me that the three weeks
> from 17 Tammuz to 9 Av are hinted at in [the book
> of] Daniel, inasmuch as Daniel fasted for three
> weeks, and it is required to refrain from meat." The
> book of Daniel contains a reference to the three
> weeks between 17 Tammuz and 9 Av in regard to
> the prohibition of eating meat. The origin of this
> fragment is from "Yakar," which is itself connected
> to Rashi's circle, and if the Rav himself converses
> with a certain Saadiah, it is certain that this Saadiah
> was French. This reading passed from *Liqqutei ha-
> Pardes* to the *Rokeah*, chap. 311 (*Ha-Rokeah ha-Gadol*,
> p. 179, ed. Shneursohn, p. 179), wherein the word
> "to me" fell out, and from there it passed to *Shibbo-
> lei ha-Leqet*, who added the title "Gaon" to the name
> Saadiah (p. 263). As to [the commentary] wrongly
> attributed [to Rav] Saadiah [Gaon],[19] it is no differ-
> ent than [the case of the book of Chronicles, which
> has] a commentary wrongly attributed to Rashi. As
> to the first, it is not impossible that it is the creation
> of Saadiah of Narbonne. . . . As to the statement

regarding the custom of refraining from meat during the Three Weeks, it is found in *Ha-Pardes* (ed. Constantinople, p. 41a; ed. Warsaw, chap. 155), and also in *Maaseh ha-Geonim*, ed. Epstein-Friedmann, chap. 49 (p. 34), and in two of the fragments it is written as well: "Rav Saadiah said to me." Therefore, there is no reason to doubt the conclusion [of the existence of a French scholar named Saadiah].[20]

As a fitting conclusion to all this, we may now add the words of Rav Saadiah Gaon himself to our discussion of the three weeks mentioned in the book of Daniel and their connection with the custom of observing the Three Weeks before Tisha Be-Av. In the commentary to the book published by R. Y. Kafih, p. 161, we find in reference to Daniel 10:2–3:

> Some have thought that these three weeks are from 17 Tammuz till 9 Av, and this is *a blatant error* for several reasons. First, the dates of 17 Tammuz and 9 Av are dates relating to the destruction of the Second Temple only, [and Daniel was mourning the destruction of the *First* Temple]. The corresponding dates for the First Temple's destruction are *9* Tammuz and *10* Av, for the city was broken into on the ninth of Tammuz. "In the fifth month, on the tenth of the month . . . the Temple of God was burnt" (Jeremiah 52:4–12).

Here then is a case where we find attributed to Rav Saadiah Gaon something which he actually wrote against. On the other hand, along with his rejection of the connection of the custom of refraining from meat and wine to the book of Daniel, we also find evidence of the custom's existence as far back as Rav Saadiah Gaon!

It should be mentioned here, however, that even though we have found that this custom originated in an erroneous reading of a Yerushalmi, it should certainly continue to be observed, as the Meiri rules in *Magen Avot*, Inyan 20, ed. R. Y. Cohen (Jerusalem, 5749), p. 215:

> A custom without origin or reason is no custom, halakhically speaking, unless there is [involved therein] some semblance of a mitzvah, or moral teaching, or gemilut hesed or some concern for [the avoidance] of some prohibition or [the prevention of some] unethical act or moral or religious failing. [In these cases, the custom, even if it has no valid origin or original reason, should be maintained.] In any case, any ancient custom should be retained and maintained, even a leniency, so long as there is no *issur*.

The Foundation Stone[21]

The tradition regarding the Foundation Stone from which the world was created is well known, and so we read in Tosefta Kippurim 2:17: "There was a stone from the days of the early prophets called Shetiyah. . . . .R. Yose says: From it was the world founded."[22]

So too, we find in Midrash ha-Gadol: "Some say that

He created His world weft and woof. From where did He begin? From the Foundation Stone, from which it was founded."[23]

One gathers from this description that there was a central point of creation from which the world spun out and spread out. However, it is difficult to combine the two images of expansion and weaving, since weaving does not begin with a central point. It seems therefore that the noun Shetiyah and the verb *hushtah* or *nishtah*, which are used in Midrash ha-Gadol and Tosefta according to the correct readings, refer not to "founding" but to the straightening of the threads used in weaving, which constitutes the first stage of the weaving process. The threads are straightened from the coil and then are tied to the loom. See, for example, the description of the process in *Spinning and Weaving in Palestine* by Sheagh Wier.[24]

We find a similar description in Midrash Tehillim 91:6,[25] where the Foundation Stone is associated with the "navel" of the world.[26]

Again, in Genesis Rabbah[27] we read: "How did the Holy One, blessed be He, create the world? Said R. Yohanan: The Holy One, blessed be He, took two coils, one of fire and one of snow, and intertwined them, and from them He created the world."

Here, the image is one of straightening two threads, perhaps of different colors, one of fire and one of snow, which is, of course, made from water, since the word *shammayim*, "heaven," is interpreted midrashically as containing the word *mayyim*, "water."

And, so too, in the Bavli, Hagigah 12a. "When the Holy One, blessed be He, wished to create the world, He unwound two coils of weft until He rebuked them and said: 'Enough.'" Here too the coils unwind until the Holy One, blessed be He, calls a stop.

Notes

1. *Minhagei Yisrael*, pp. 138–146.
2. Yerushalmi Taanit 1:6 (66c), Yerushalmi Pesahim 4:1 (30d).
3. In most sources, eating meat generally precedes the mention of drinking wine, as in the sugya in Taanit mentioned above, and so the reversal of this order indicates that "eating meat" is an addition to the original text; it was *added* to the first clause, and so does not precede the wine here as it does elsewhere. The phenomenon is known from many other sources, and at times we can follow the process in the manuscripts; in one manuscript the addition is completely absent, in another it is written in the margin or between the lines, and in the next it has entered the text, but not in a natural place.
4. See Addendum at the end of this chapter.
5. See also *Pardes*, siman 260; *Siddur Rashi*, siman 405, pp. 203 f.
6. See *Mafteah to Megillat Setarim*, siman 63, ed. S. Asaf; *Tarbiz* 11, p. 252; ed. S. Abramson, *Rav Nissim Gaon* (Jerusalem, 5725), p. 274.
7. The same reading can be found in *Seridei Yerushalmi* (a collection of manuscript fragments), p. 111, and in *Yalqut ha-Makhiri* to Psalms 11:5, p. 67.
8. See S. Lieberman, *Ha-Yerushalmi ki-fshuto*, pp. 430-431.
9. As the *Sedeh Yehoshua* remarks, cited by R. S. Lieberman in *Yerushalmi ki-fshuto* there. In the meantime, of course, the custom has expanded to include men as well. However,

even as late as the time of the Maharshal (sixteenth century), he could write in his responsa (siman 24) that the custom was for "women not to eat meat in these three weeks."

10. Ed. Auerbach, vol. 2, p. 12.
11. The Meiri's *Magen Avot*, Inyan 20, end 98.
12. See Y. Kutscher, "Itzurei ha-Garon ba-Galil," in *Mehqarim
be-Ivrit uve-Aramit*, pp. 210 f., with additions in his *Studies
in Galilean Aramaic*, ed. M. Sokoloff (Ramat Gan, 1976), p.
105.
13. Genesis 25:21.
14. Despite all this, R. Lieberman is of the opinion that the
custom not to drink wine during the Nine Days was prevalent in Eretz Israel; see his *Ha-Yerushalmi ki-fshuto*. However, I have yet to find proof for this view. And even if
such a custom existed, the connection of the Yerushalmi
we have discussed with this later custom is still erroneous.
15. Or perhaps strengthened an originally existent custom; see
the preceding note and Tur, O.H. 551: "There are variants
which read 'not to eat meat or drink wine,' and from this
comes the custom not to eat meat or drink wine in the
week [during which Tisha Be-Av falls], and some add [the
days] from Rosh Hodesh until the fast [of Tisha Be-Av]."
16. As for the original custom for women not to spin or weave
during this time, we may connect it with the common phenomenon in many cultures that women do not weave in
times of trouble, perhaps because one ought not to *begin* to
manufacture new clothing at such times; see J. Frazer, *The
New Golden Bough*, ed. Theodor H. Gaster (Stanford, 1964),
p. 173.

The original custom is *also* found in Shulhan Arukh,
O.H. 551:4: "Women who are accustomed not to spin [i.e.,
to arrange the threads which go lengthwise through the
garment, from the words *sheti va-erev*, 'weft and wool']
wool from when Av arrives . . ."

17. Literally: "Weeks of days."
18. See "Qetaim mi-Divrei Rasag," *Sefer Rav Saadiah Gaon—Qovetz Torani-Mada'i*, ed. R. Y. L. Fishman (Jerusalem, 5703), p. 307.
19. Known as "pseudo-Saadiah"—on the book of Daniel.
20. It now appears that its source may be Greek; see Y. Ta-Shema, *Tarbiz* 55 (5746): 65.
21. *Minhagei Yisrael*, pp. 147–148.
22. See R. Shaul Lieberman, *Tosefta ki-fshutah*, vol. 4 (New York, 5722), pp. 772–773, and see my book, *Midrash Yerushalayim* (Jerusalem, 1982), pp. 66, 70. On the correct reading in Tosefta Kippurim 2:14, see Lieberman's edition, p. 238, l. 118, and see also Louis Ginzberg's erudite collection, *Legends of the Jews*, vol. 1, p. 15.
23. *Midrash ha-Gadol*, ed. Margulies, p. 12, and see Lieberman (n. 22 above).
24. (London: British Museum, 1970), p. 14.
25. Ed. Buber, p. 400.
26. See Lieberman, p. 773.
27. Ed. Theodor-Albeck, p. 75.

PART VII
ROSH HASHANAH

CHAPTER 13[1]
ותוציא לאור משפטינו היום–איום–קדוש

AT TIMES A SLIGHT CHANGE of wording, or even the change
of a single letter, can reveal the broad dimensions of a
disagreement between different schools of thought regarding the proper shape and form of *tefillah*. An example of this may be found in the discussion about the
proper wording of the conclusion to HaYom Harat
Olam, which comes after *teqiot* on Rosh Hashanah.[2]

The version in our current *mahzorim* usually runs as
follows: עד שתחננו ותוציא כאור משפטינו היום (נ׳א איום) קדוש,
"until You show us mercy, [clear and pure] as the light,
and issue our verdict today, Holy One".[3]

141

Now, in the Provençal version of the *mahzor*, recorded in *Sefer ha-Manhig*, Hilkhot Rosh Hashanah, siman 23,
ed. Raael, p. 327, we have the following:

ותוציא לאור⁴ משפטינו קדוש. ותוציא says whoever and ,ותוציא
היום משפטינו לאור has not arranged his prayers
properly, for we should not be seen to consider
ourselves to be like the totally righteous who[se
names] are immediately recorded in the Book of
Life, but rather like those in between, who are held
in suspense until Yom Kippur. This is [the tradi-
tion] I received in France.⁵

It seems that this version, without the word היום, "today," is the version of Rashi's school.⁶

עד שתחננו ותוציא לאור משפטינו קדוש. The word היום
should not be said, since we cannot be sure that our
verdict will be issued before Yom Kippur, since the
whole matter depends on [our] repentance. And
should you say, "But are not the righteous sealed
immediately for life?" Do you really think that we
should consider ourselves totally righteous people?

The same sentiments are expressed in *Mahzor Vitry*.⁷
Thus we see that the Sages of France were prepared
to change the wording of this *piyyut*, eliminating a word
(or adding a word), in order to make the *tefillah* conform
to halakhic sources.

On the other hand, the Sages of Germany, and in
particular those under the influence of the Hasidei Ash-

kenaz, the circle of R. Yehudah he-Hasid, could not permit themselves such changes, since they held that the words and letters of the prayers were carefully counted in accordance with mystical considerations. Any change might have catastrophic consequences in regard to the hidden intentions hinted at by these numbers. We find sharp words directed against these practices in R. Yehudah he-Hasid's commentary to the *mahzor* of Rosh Hashanah, cited in *Siddur R. Shelomoh b. R. Shimon of Worms*, ed. R. M. Hershler (Jerusalem, 5732), siman 99, p. 221—immediately after the commentary to HaYom Harat Olam.

> The *tefillah* of Rosh Hashanah is composed in order, and we may not add or subtract even one word, for it is as copied from the son of R. Eleazar ha-Gadol, R. Yehudah he-Hasid's own copy of his commentary. . . . And whoever adds or subtracts *even one letter*, his prayer is not heard [on High], for all of it is carefully weighed and measured *by word and letter*, with many secrets involved [in these calculations]. Whoever fears God must not subtract or add, *and one should not listen to the French* and the inhabitants of the seacoast, who add several words, for the Sages are not pleased with [such activities, or with the people who engage in them], and the reasons for the [wording of] the prayers and the secrets [involved in them] were not handed down to them. For the early Hasidim would hide away the secrets and reasons, until our Holy Teacher, Rabbenu Yehudah Hasid, ז״ל, handed them down to

the men of his family, the Hasidim, in writing and orally.

It is clear that his intent is to warn against the school of Rashi, the "French," who, because of their lack of knowledge of the hints of the secrets of *tefillah*, would change the wording, ruining the hidden *kavvanot* implicit in the number of words and letters.

In regard to our issue, we find the following (ibid., p. 227):

> I have heard that R. Yaakov [= Rabbenu Tam] would eliminate the word היום from *mahzorim*, but he would say ותוציא לאור משפטינו קדוש, because the verdict of the wicked is not complete on Rosh Hashanah, but rather suspended until Yom Kippur. It may be that he said this, but he must not have known that there are thirty-two words in HaYom Harat, corresponding to the thirty-two Ways with which the world was created, . . . and the thirty-two words from "let us make man" until "male and female He created them," as well as many other [correspondences] which my teacher, Rabbenu he-Hasid ז״ל, laid down, giving a reason and a secret for each one. . . . Therefore, one who fears God should be careful not to add or subtract.

How severe was the complaint of the German Sages against the French Sages, led by Rabbenu Tam, to whom, apparently, the secrets and hints of the prayers had not been handed down!

There were those, however, who attempted to bridge the gap between the mystical claims of the Hasidei Ashkenaz and the halakhic arguments of the French Sages. R. Avraham b. R. Azriel, in his *Arugat ha-Bosem* (ed. Urbach, vol. 3, p. 474) suggested the following:

היום הרת עולם—there are thirty-two words in this *piyyut*, corresponding to the thirty-two Ways by which the world was created, as is noted in *Sefer Yetzirah* [1:1]. One should not say: ותוציא.לאור משפטינו קדוש [leaving out the word היום], for then a word will be missing, as is explained in *Siddur Rashi*, Seder Rosh Hashanah.[8] Instead, we should say: ותוציא לאור משפטינו האל קדוש.

Here we find a compromise: the suggestion of the French Sages to omit the word "today" is accepted, but in order not to change the number of words, another word is substituted, האל.

However, this was not sufficient to satisfy the complaint of R. Yehudah he-Hasid, since he emphasized the importance not only of the words, but also of the *letters*. Such a substitution as suggested in *Arugat ha-Bosem* yields one less letter in HaYom Harat. It seems, therefore, that another version was created to meet this objection: the substitution of the word איום ("Fearful One") for היום ("today"), both of which have four letters.[9] In addition, the word sounds almost identical to היום; indeed, if the tradition of R. Yehudah he-Hasid had been transmitted orally, it would have been easy to connect the new version with the old tradition, and thus to justify it, or even to see it as the original wording of R. Yehudah he-Hasid.[10]

There is another aspect to this issue that is worthy of examination. The French Sages based their emendation on the famous Talmudic passage in Rosh Hashanah 16b:

> Said R. Yohanan: Three books are opened on Rosh Hashanah: one for the totally wicked, one for the totally righteous, and one for the intermediates. The totally righteous are entered and sealed for life immediately; the totally wicked are entered and sealed for death immediately; the intermediates are suspended from Rosh Hashanah to Yom Kippur. If they merit [it], they are entered for life; if not, for death.[11]

However, the opinion of R. Yohanan is not the only one found among Hazal; there are in all four different views on the matter, as cited in the Yerushalmi Rosh Hashanah 1:3.[12]

> Some teach: All of them are judged on Rosh Ha-shanah, *and the verdict of each one is sealed on Rosh Hashanah.*
>
> Others teach: All of them are judged on Rosh Hashanah, and the verdict of each one is sealed on Yom Kippur.
>
> Still others teach: All of them are judged on Rosh Hashanah, and the verdict of each one is sealed in its own time.
>
> Still others teach: Each one is judged in his time,

and the verdict of each one is sealed in its time.

The opinion of Rav says: All of them are judged on Rosh Hashanah, and the verdict of each one is sealed on Rosh Hashanah, for it is taught in the *teqiot* of Rav: "This is the day of the beginning of Your creations, a remembrance of the First Day, for it is a law in Israel, a judgment of the God of Jacob. And regarding the countries it is said on it: Which one for the sword, which one for peace, which one for famine, and which one for plenty. *And the creatures are judged to be mentioned for life and for death.*[13]

Thus, according to the opinion of the "first tanna" in the Yerushalmi's baraita, and also according to Rav, according to the Yerushalmi's understanding, the verdict for each individual is sealed on Rosh Hashanah, and our *piyyut*, HaYom Harat Olam ("today is the birth of the world"),[14] goes according to Rav, who, like R. Eliezer, holds on the matter of Creation that the world was created in Tishrei (Rosh Hashanah 27a). Thus the *piyyut* is consistent in following Rav, and so, in the end, Rabbenu Tam's emendation may be called into question, and there is no reason to emend the *piyyut*.

Notes

1. *Minhagei Yisrael*, vol. 1, pp. 121–124, and vol. 2, pp. 272–273.
2. This prayer is found in all communities, and dates back at least to Geonic times; though it is not found in *Siddur Rasag* (Rav Saadiah Gaon), it is found in *Seder Rav Amram Gaon*, pt. II, siman 114, ed. Goldschmidt (Jerusalem, 5732),

p. 142, though its connection to Rav Amram's Gaon's *seder* is not altogether clear.

3. See, for example, *Mahzor le-Yomim Noraim*, Rosh Hashanah, ed. D. Goldschmidt (Jerusalem, 5730), p. 244, l. 5, and the editor's notes there.

4. We will not enter here into the question of the difference between לאור and כאור; see Goldschmidt's notes.

5. See the notes on l. 4, where the variant "in the name of R. Sh.ז״ל " is added.

6. See *Siddur Rashi*, siman 181, pp. 83–84.

7. Siman 335, p. 372.

8. This is not in *Siddur Rashi* as we have it; see the editor's notes there.

9. See Goldschmidt's edition of the *mahzor*, in the variant readings for line 5. The version היום is found in ten manuscripts, eight from a group stemming from western Germany (see Introduction, pp. 51–52), and two from *Minhag Tzorfat*, from the French custom (ibid., p. 53); thus this version was known in France, but was later eliminated. There are another thirteen manuscripts following the French version (ibid., pp. 53–54) in which the word is missing, and they reflect Rabbenu Tam's emendation. The change to איום can be found in manuscripts originating in the area of AF"M (Asti, Fossano, and Moncalvo, in the Piedmonte region of northern Italy, to which French refugees went; see Goldschmidt, p. 13), not earlier than the eighteenth century (ibid., p. 54). It is clear, therefore, that this is a new version.

10. On emendations and corrections in *mahzorim*, see what I wrote in *Bibliotheca Orientalis* 42 (1985): 382, and see *Magen Avot* of the Meiri, Inyan Rishon, ed. R. Y. Cohen (Jerusalem, 5749), p. 40.

11. This in turn is based on the teaching of Beth Shammai, which is also recorded in the Talmud there. "It has been

taught: Beth Shammai say: There will be three groups on the Day of Judgment: one of the totally righteous, one of the totally wicked, and one of the intermediates. The totally righteous will be immediately entered for everlasting life; the totally wicked will be immediately entered for Gehenna, as it is written: 'And many of them that sleep in the dust of the earth will awake, some to everlasting life and some to reproaches and everlasting abhorrence' (Daniel 12:2). The intermediate will go down to Gehenna and squeal and rise again, as it is written: 'And I will bring the third part through the fire, and will refine them as silver is refined, and will try them as gold is tried. They shall call on My Name and I will answer them' (Zechariah 13:9). Of them Hannah said: 'The Lord kills and brings to life, He brings down to the grave and brings up' (I Samuel 2:6)."

12. See Tosefta Rosh Hashanah 1:3, ed. Lieberman, p. 308, and Rosh Hashanah 16a, where the first opinion does not appear.

13. In the continuation: And this is not according to R. Yose's opinion, for R. Yose said: An individual is judged every hour. What is the reason? "You judge us every morning, every moment you test us" (Job 7:18). Compare the Bavli there.

14. See Goldschmidt's comment in his *Mahzor le-Yom ha-Kippurim*, p. 244, l. 1, and see his Introduction, p. 28.

CHAPTER 14[1]
One Hundred Teqiot

WE HAVE ALREADY SEEN that numbers and numerology play a large role in connection with all sorts of customs, especially those dealing with *tefillah*. This may explain an otherwise difficult matter, the tradition cited by the Geonim regarding the *teqiot* that are sounded on Rosh Hashanah. It is reported in the name of the Yerushalmi, or what "the Westerners say," that the hundred *teqiot* which we sound correspond to the hundred shrieks or wails which Sisera's mother shrieked.[2]

This refers, of course, to the story in the Song of Deborah (Judges 5:28): "Through the window she looked, the mother of Sisera wailed (ותיבב) through the latticework, Why has his chariot delayed in coming? Why do the sounds of his chariot tarry?"

Since *teqiot* are called *yebavot* (יבבות), the Talmud already connected the wails of Sisera's mother with the *teqiot*; Abaye expounded, "It shall be a day of *teruah* ["shofar blowing"] for you" (Numbers 29:1), which we translate (into Aramaic) as "A day of יבבא shall it be for you," and it is further written regarding Sisera's mother, "Through the window she looked, and she wailed," etc.

Nevertheless, the question arises as to where the tradition of a "hundred wails" originates. The *derashah*, which is not to be found in the Yerushalmi available to us, seems merely to be a "midrash" quoted in various places but with no firm source, as B. M. Lewin suggested.[3]

However, in Tanhuma Emor 11 we find the second half of Isaiah 41:24 expounded as follows: "[But you are less than naught,] and your doings are naught (ופעלכם מאפע)"—less than the hundred wails which a woman wails in labor, ninety-nine for death and one for life," thus connecting אפע with פעיה. *Etz Yosef* interprets the midrash as a play on מאפע, with a rearrangement of the letters to מפע א׳, one wail of a hundred, with the hundred coming from yet another rearrangement, מא[ה] פע[יות], "one hundred wails." The theme of a hundred wails was then transferred to the wails of Sisera's mother.

The question then arises as to the origin of the number one hundred to begin with. The two verses in Judges (5:28–29) from the Song of Deborah, which each contain a hundred letters, would seem to have been the source of this midrash, and thus, by extension, of the tradition of one hundred shofar blasts on Rosh Hashanah.

Notes
1. From *Minhagei Yisrael*, vol. 2, pp. 181–182.

2. See *Arukh*, s.v. *ayin-resh-bet* I; *Arukh ha-Shalem*, vol. 10, p. 249b (and see the editor's comment, n. 9). Parallels, with changes, can be found in the *Pardes*, ed. Ehrenreich, pp. 219–220, at the end of Rabbenu Hananel to Rosh Hashanah, etc. See all this in *Otzar ha-Geonim* to Rosh Hashanah, pp. 89 f., "Quntras Erbuv ha-Satan be-Rosh Hashanah."
3. *Otzar ha-Geonim*, p. 92. However, see *Torah Shelemah*, vol. 4 (Hayyei Sarah), pp. 920–921, n. 17; R. Kasher wished to emend this "midrash" as follows: "Corresponding to the hundred wails which our mother Sarah wailed," following the Yemenite *Hemdat Yamim*. His suggestion seems forced; see also S. Spiegel, *The Last Trial* (New York, 1969), pp. 74–75, n. 42.

CHAPTER 15[1]
The Prohibition of Eating Nuts on Rosh Hashanah

THE REMA, IN HIS NOTES to Shulhan Arukh, Orah Hayyim
583:2, cites the custom not to eat nuts on the night of
Rosh Hashanah,[2] since the Hebrew word for "nut," אגוז,
is equivalent to חטא, "sin," in *gematria*.[3] Another reason
given is that nuts increase phlegm and interfere with
praying.[4]

Hayyim Leshem, in his important book *Shabbat
u-Moadei Yisrael ba-Halakhah, ba-Aggadah, be-Historiyah,
ve-Havvay, ube-Folklore* (Tel Aviv, 5729), pp. 11–114, investigated the folkloristic aspects of the roots of this custom. For example, ancient scholars viewed the nut as a
symbol of destruction and harm; "since the shade and
moisture of a nut tree caused harm to the trees surrounding it, lexicographers derived the Latin word for
'nut,' *nux*, from *nocere*, 'to harm, destroy.'" This idea is

first noted by Isadore of Seville, who died in 636, and R. Yosef Kimhi cites it in his commentary on Song of Songs 6:11, "I went down to a nut garden." Kimhi interprets it as follows: "The wicked kingdom is symbolized by a nut, because a nut tree causes irreparable harm to whatever trees its shade blankets. So too the wicked kingdom harms and destroys the Jews, who are compared to a vine and pomegranate.[5]

Leshem cites other negative traditions about the nut, but he also cites a large number of positive comments, among them a midrash in Shir ha-Shirim Rabba 6:

> Just as a nut, if it falls into mud, you may pick it up, wash it, and clean it, and it retains its original purity, and is good to eat, so too Israel; however they become muddied with sin all year round, [when] Yom Kippur comes upon them [they become pure].

If so, however, we might expect that the eating of nuts on Rosh Hashanah and during the rest of the Yomim Noraim would be recommended rather than prohibited, since they symbolize forgiveness and repentance!

Leshem suggests that it may have been precisely this conundrum which motivated the use of the *gematria* as an additional reason for forbidding the eating of nuts, since nuts have both positive and negative associations, in order to promote the prohibition of eating nuts from Rosh Hashanah till after Hoshana Rabba.[6]

Here we wish to explain this riddle in another way, one which derives from the other consideration cited by

Rema, namely, the increase in phlegm that eating nuts produces.

In the Maharil, Hilkhot Rosh Hashanah, ed. Spitzer (Jerusalem, 5749), p. 287, siman 2 (see the editor's n. 3):

Mahari Segal expounded: Everyone should take care not to spit out [phlegm] at the time of blowing the shofar; similarly, it seems that [one should refrain] from what is called *raeuspern* [= clearing one's throat], in order that the sound of the shofar should be heard from start to finish without even the slightest[7] interruption. . . . Therefore, anything which produces phlegm should not be eaten on Rosh Hashanah, and for this reason people are careful not to eat nuts on Rosh Hashanah before shofar-blowing,[8] because it increases moisture.

It would seem that they were concerned about this because on Rosh Hashanah people were accustomed to eat special foods as a "good sign," as explained in Tur, O.H. 583, and so they were particularly concerned *not* to eat foods which were considered unsuitable for one reason or another; as a result these foods came to be considered "forbidden."

The source for the custom of eating special foods is explained in the Tur, based on Keritot 6a.

Said Abaye: Now that you have said that a "sign" is considered a matter of importance, a person should habituate himself to eat at the beginning of the year: citron, pumpkin, fenugreek, leek, beet, and dates

(אתרוגא קרי רוביא כרתי סלקי ותמרי רוביא).[9] Rashi explains [several as plays on words]: תלתן רוביא—ירבו זכויתינו, ruvya—may our merits be increased,[10] kartei—may our [enemies or sins] be cut off,[11] . . . . pumpkins, because they grow quickly. And from this have grown various customs, each place according to its own custom. For example, in Germany, where they are accustomed to eat before the meal sweet apples dipped in honey, one should say: "May the new year be sweet." And in Provence, where they are accustomed to place on their tables all sorts of new things,[12] and they eat the head of a sheep and lungs, saying: "Let us be a head [= leaders, respected people] and not a tail [= people of no account]." And the lung because it is light [to digest]. The [Maha]ram of Rothenburg was accustomed to eat the head of a male ram as a symbol of Isaac's ram.

Since various communities sought to find "all sorts of new things," they were also careful to avoid foods which in their opinion were unsuitable for Rosh Hasha-nah, and gave reasons for their "prohibitions." So it seems from the words of the Rema in Shulhan Arukh, O.H. 583:5, where R. Yosef Karo wrote: "They eat a sheep's head," and Rema comments: "Some are careful not to eat nuts, etc."

Moreover, some authorities rejected the gematria.

That which some say, that we should not eat nuts on Rosh Hashanah because nuts in gematria are equivalent to "sin"—there is nothing to it, for what

do we have to do with *gematriyot*? According to
them, we should be permitted to eat hazelnuts, for
in Hebrew they are called *luzim*, [and thus have a
different *gematria*]. But the [real] reason is so as not
to increase phlegm to the point that one would be
unable to pray. And for this reason even hazelnuts
would be prohibited.[13]

He was not the only one to question the *gematria*,
which troubled others. First of all, as noted above, it is
not complete, since the word חטא must be spelled without the *alef* in order for it to work. Moreover, other, positive *gematriyot* are available for "nut"—the word טוב,
"good," for example.[14] Again, it is strange that the Rema
lists this as his primary reason, while relegating the
phlegm reason to secondary status.

The Hatam Sofer, in his notes to the Shulhan Arukh,
makes the following comments:

Some are careful not to eat nuts, for "nut" is equivalent to "sin" in *gematria*, and moreover, they increase phlegm. It seems to me, in my poor view,
that the reason is that Hazal commented on the
verse "To a nut garden" (Song of Songs 6:11): Why
is Israel compared to a nut? Just as a nut's fruit
does not become muddy even when it rolls in a
muddy place, for its interior does not become
repugnant, so too Israel, even when they wander
among the nations of the world, their center does
not become repugnant. And since the nut signifies
exile, it is not proper to eat it on Rosh Hashanah.

Moreover, the initial letters of the words of the beginning of Leviticus 26:44: ואף גם זאת—"and despite
this [I will not reject them when they are in the land
of their enemies]." אף גם זאת—*alef gimmel zayyin*.[15]

R. Yosef Hann Neuerlingen, in *Yosef Ometz* (Frankfurt am Main, 5688; reprint ed., Jerusalem, 5725), siman
977, p. 217, writes:

Whoever refrains from nuts, the essential reason is
in order not to come to coughing and clearing one's
throat during the blowing of the shofar, thus causing others to miss some of the *teqiot*. Therefore, on
the second day of Rosh Hashanah after midday, it
is permitted.

And, indeed, in *Sefer Zikhron Avraham*, by R. Avraham Bing, a student of R. Nathan Adler[16] (Pressburg,
5652), siman 583, he writes regarding his teacher, that he
never saw him reprove a student for eating nuts on the
second day of Rosh Hashanah after midday.[17]

It is surprising that the Rema himself listed the *gematria* as the first, and presumably primary, reason for the
prohibition, while the Maharil's suggestion, that the prohibition was to reduce the coughing and clearing of
throats during prayers, he cites as only an additional
reason. First of all, the *gematria* does not completely
work, as noted; it is difficult to say that the *alef* "does not
count." Though it is often the case that *gematriyot* are
"off" by one, this is hardly the *gematria* on which one

would care to base a prohibition, especially when a more cogent reason exists.

It is therefore no surprise that *Noheg ka-Tzon Yosef* rejected this with the harsh comment that *"there is nothing to it."* Rema's comment becomes all the more surprising when we remember that his general policy is to give rationalistic reasons for customs which cannot be easily explained in a rational way. For example, in his explanation of Tashlich, the Rema provides an allegorical-rationalistic reason in his *Torah ha-Olah* (pt. III, chap. 56), in place of the more usual kabbalistic-mystical one.[18]

In order to answer these questions we must return to the roots of these matters. We have already seen above that the custom arose because of a concern for positive "signs" for the new year, and each community adopted different foods to make this essential point. Some made fruit the central symbol, some used vegetables, and some chose various types of meat. Some chose foods whose names could serve as plays on words in expressing a wish for the new year—*seleq,* "beet," שיסתלקו אויבינו —"[May it be God's will] that our enemies depart." At times the shape of the food gave rise to the symbol, as in the case of the sheep's head—"that we be at the head and not at the tail."

This being the case, nearly any food could serve the purpose and find a place in the festive meal, and carry its symbolic freight in one way or another, so long as it was food appropriate for a festival and had something new about it. At times even nuts served the purpose, as

in the time of the Maharam of Rothenberg, of whom the
Kolbo reports that "the [Maha]ram was accustomed to,
and *did not refrain from, eating* garlic and nuts or anything else."[19] This fact was known to the Rema, who
cited the *Kolbo* in *Darkei Moshe*. Certainly, it was possible
to provide a suitably festive symbol for the nut; they
may even have served nuts dipped in honey as a symbol
of a sweet coming year, as was customary in those
days.[20] However, the Maharil was concerned not to eat
foods which would interfere with the proper recital of
the Rosh Hashanah prayers by producing phlegm, thus
interfering with listening to the shofar-blowing.[21]
Among these foods were nuts, and the Rema accepted
this opinion.

Now, the custom of eating foods symbolizing good
wishes for the new year has its origin in the Talmud, but
the two places in which Abaye's statement appears differ slightly. In Horayot 12a we have:

> Said Abaye: Now that you have said that a "sign"
> is considered a matter of importance, a person
> should habituate himself to *see* at the beginning of
> the year: pumpkin, fenugreek, leek, beet, and dates
> (קרא רוביא כרתי סלקי ותמרי רוביא).

whereas in Keritot 6a we have:

> Said Abaye: Now that you have said that a "sign"
> is considered a matter of importance, a person
> should habituate himself to *eat* at the beginning of

the year: citron, pumpkin, fenugreek, leek, beet,
and dates (אתרוגא קרא רוביא כרתי סלקי ותמרי רוביא).

The essential difference is, of course, the variant
"eat/see."

The *Arukh* also had the variant "see,"[22] as did *Mahzor Vitry*, siman 323, p. 362; the Meiri in *Hibbur ha-Teshuvah*, p. 265; *Shibbolei ha-Leqet*, siman 283, p. 266; etc. The
Bet Yosef had both versions.

There was also a third interpretation, if not version.
Sefer ha-Manhig writes: "Now that you have said that a
'sign' is considered a matter of importance, a person
should habituate himself to *hold* at the beginning of the
year . . . "[23] As the editor correctly notes, the custom
seems to have been *to take hold of each species*, but not to
eat any of them.[24]

This custom dates back to Geonic times. We have a
report that Rav Hai Gaon would take hold of each
species and say the proper prayer; his students would
then take the fruits and vegetables home.[25] Incidentally,
Rav Hai would use honey as well as the Talmud's rec-
ommendations.

Similar customs are reported by *Halakhot Gedolot*,[26]
where the head of the house would *look at and place his
hand on* the fruit or vegetable and recite the prayer. In
later centuries the Meiri and *Orhot Hayyim* report similar
customs.[27]

Understandably, many had the "to eat" version and
did eat the symbolic foods.[28] For those who ate them,
then, it was proper to warn them to refrain from eating

nuts and to explain why: to prevent interference with the shofar-blowing or prayers, by people clearing their throats. On the other hand, for those who merely held or viewed these symbolic foods while reciting a prayer based on the association of sound or shape, no such warning was necessary, and the association of nuts was positive. However, for those who ate the symbolic foods, such an association was not possible, and what better way to prevent this than to produce a *negative* association, such as a *gematria* which associated nuts with sin, even when a better *gematria* existed for the positive side (nuts = good)? In this mindset of symbolic acts, what better way to prevent an undesirable result than to use the very psychology which was at work? Thus, the Rema, who ordinarily did not resort to *gematriyot*, did so in this case.

Why should the Rema have extend the prohibition even to those whose custom was not to eat the nuts but merely to hold them or show them to those at the meal? Presumably, once the nuts were at table, they would be eaten at some point, if only not to violate the prohibition of *bal tashhit* against wasting or misusing useful objects. Even if the nuts were not eaten at the first meal, they would be eaten sometime during the festival, possibly before the shofar blowing. And so the Rema adopted the Maharil's prohibition and added the *gematria* to give it weight, not only for those who ate them, but even for those who merely showed them but might come to eat them later.

My colleague and good friend, Prof. Shamma

Friedman, kindly gave me an as yet unpublished article of his, due to appear in the forthcoming *Sefer ha-Yovel for Prof. Shelomo Morag*, edited by Prof. Moshe Bar-Asher et al., in which I found a comment which touches directly on the problematical *gematria* of אגוז and חטא.

> Kutscher already noted that this *gematria* "is based on the spelling חט, which is common in early rabbinic manuscripts," noting in particular the Vatican manuscript of the Sifra.[29] But it is more likely to suppose that this spelling was known to the later Rishonim in Germany, given its currency in Germany, and in particular in German manuscripts of the Bavli and others associated with them,[30] than to assume that the spelling came from the East or Eretz Yisrael. The omission of the *alef* in words such as ברי is much more common in the [German] Florence . . . manuscripts [of the Bavot] than in the [Spanish] Hamburg manuscript, which prefers [the fuller spelling,] בריא.

Prof. Friedman's assumption regarding the spelling חט in Ashkenaz may more easily explain the addition of the *gematria* as an additional reason for forbidding the eating of nuts on Rosh Hashanah.

Notes

1. *Minhagei Yisrael*, vol. 4, pp. 41–49; see also vol. 2, p. 191.
2. Since eating in the morning before Shaharit is prohibited, the essential prohibition of nuts must pertain to the night before.

3. According to the value of the letters; א = 1 + ג = 3+ ו = 6+ ז = 7 = 17 = ח = 8 + ט = 9 + (א = 1), spelling *het* without the *alef*.

4. See also *Darkei Moshe* to Tur, O.H. 583:1.

5. See Berliner's *Magazin* 6 (1879): 159–160.

6. *Shabbat u-Moadei Yisrael*, p. 114, and see pp. 313–315 in regard to lentils.

7. Literally: of a thread's breadth.

8. That is, the night before, since eating before hearing the shofar is forbidden in any case.

9. Compare the parallel text in Horiyot 12a, where it states that a person should "see," not necessarily eat. The various differences between the two Talmudic sources have been discussed by the Rishonim; see *Mahzor Vitry*, p. 362, n. 2; *Sefer ha-Manhig*, ed. Rafael, p. 304; n. 58; see next note.

10. The word "increase," *yirbu*, is signaled by the word *ruvya*.

11. Both are related to the root כרת, "to cut off."

12. This is the expression used by the Manhig, Hilkhot Rosh Hashanah, siman 1, ed. Rafael, p. 304.

13. R. Juspa Kashman Segal, *Sefer Noheg ka-Tzon Yosef* (Tel Aviv, 5729), pp. 270–271, n. 18.

14. This was pointed out in an addition to Rashi's comment to Isaiah 1:1 in a *Miqraot Gedolot* printed in Amsterdam, 1699, added by "R. Ovadiah the Prophet," on whom see the illuminating article by R. Hayyim Lieberman in *Ohel Rahel*, vol. 1 (New York, 5740), pp. 310–329.

15. Perhaps the *vav* of ואף is also part of the word אומר.

16. The Hatam Sofer's teacher as well.

17. See "Peninei Moadim," there.

18. See *Minhagei Yisrael*, vol. 3, pp. 120–121, n. 23.

19. See *Tashbetz ha-Qatan*, siman 118; *Orhot Hayyim* pt. I, siman 5; Abudarham, Seder ha-Tefillot shel Rosh Hashanah, p. 98, etc. See also *Teshuvot Pesaqim u-Minhagim shel ha-Maharam me-Rottenberg*, ed. Kahana, vol. 1 (Jerusalem, 5717), p. 296, siman 522, and the notes there. From this report of the

Maharam's custom it is clear that others did refrain from eating nuts.

20. See *Orhot Hayyim*, Hilkhot Berakhot, siman 27, p. 85; *Mahzor Vitry*, siman 73, p. 40; *Shibbolei ha-Leqet*, siman 163; *Siddur Rashi*, siman 122, pp. 59–60; *Pardes*, siman 77; Tosafot (misattributed to) R. Yehudah "Hasid" to Berakhot 38b, ed. Zaks, p. 422; *Semag*, Asin 27; *Or Zarua*, vol. 1, siman 168; *Agudah*, Berakhot chap. 6, siman 134, *Semaq*, siman 151, *Hagahot Maimuniyot*, Hilkhot Berakhot 3, siman 5; *Agur*, siman 280, p. 57; Tur, O.H. 202, etc. Note the report of *Mahzor Vitry*: "At times I saw that they would bring before my master nuts fried in honey. . . . They called it בשטרי and made the blessing *bore peri ha-etz* on it, for he said: 'The nut is the essential part of the dish; the honey is secondary.'" In *Siddur Rashi* the sweet is called יורבעס, and Buber in his notes cites *Sefer ha-Sedarim*, in which it is called אדבעסל.

In passing, let me make note of an ancient report of the use of honey to celebrate the incoming new year, as reported in Papyrus 3812 of the Oxyrhyncus papyri from Egypt, dating from the end of the third century B.C.E. (see Ranon Katzoff in *Bulletin of the American Society of Papyrologists* 25 [1988]: 158). Katzoff is quite right in emphasizing the importance of this report in assessing the background of the medieval custom.

21. Already, Dioscorides in the first century C.E. wrote negatively regarding the walnut in his book *De Materia Medica* (chap. 1, sec. 178): "[They] are hard of digestion, they hurt the stomach, engender choler, breed headache, are nought for such as have the cough, but good to make one vomit if they be eaten by one fasting" (trans. R. T. Gunthen).

Now, *Hagahot Maimoniyyot* noted that "there are places in which [people] refrain from fasting on Erev Rosh Hashanah, because of the prohibition [of following] gentile customs (Hilkhot Shofar, siman 1, beginning). It is possible, then, that the teacher of the *Hagahot Maimoniyyot*, the Maharam of Rothenberg, did not fast on Erev Rosh Hashanah for this reason, and thus was not concerned [not] to eat nuts on the night of Rosh Hashanah." In contrast, the Maharil noted that "it is a custom in all the communities of Israel that young men and women eat nuts before dawn on Erev Yom Kippur . . . in order that they fast" (see *Sefer Maharil*, ed. Spitzer, siman 262). It would seem, then, that most people did fast on Erev Rosh Hashanah, and therefore they were careful not to eat nuts the following night. However, all this is speculative.

22. S.v. קרן, *Arukh ha-Shalem*, vol. 7, p. 183a.
23. Hilkhot Rosh Hashanah, siman 1, ed. Rafael, p. 304.
24. See n. to l. 57 there.
25. See *Otzar ha-Geonim*, Rosh Hashanah, siman 92, p. 52, quoted from *Ginzei Qedem* 3, pp. 67–68.
26. Siman 166; *Otzar Geonim*, loc. cit., siman 93, p. 53.
27. *Hibbur ha-Teshuvah*, ibid., and *Orhot Hayyim*, Hilkhot Rosh Hashanah, siman 5, p. 95b. All these sources are cited by the editor of *Sefer ha-Manhig*, ibid., together with the *Eshkol*, ed. Albeck, pt. 2, p. 94.
28. See *Ravyah*, vol. 2, siman 547, p. 247, for example, and Aptowitzer's n. 19.
29. See *Haaretz*, Feb. 14, 1962.
30. Even in the printed Talmud; see Zevahim 45a.

CHAPTER 16[1]
עושה השלום

WE HAVE ALREADY SEEN how numerological considerations led to changes in the wording of prayers. Thus, for example, the substitution of עושה השלום for המברך את עמו ישראל בשלום on Rosh Hashanah[2] is determined by a *gematria*. עושה השלום in *gematria* is equivalent to ספראל, the angel in charge of writing; we mention him until he inscribes us for a good and peaceful and life.[3]

According to the Ashenazic custom, we conclude the Blessing of Peace with עושה השלום. However, in *Siddur ha-Shelah* (Tefillat Rosh Hashanah), we are warned against such a change, even though the kabbalists are undoubtedly correct in their intent. Nevertheless, since the change is not found in the Talmud or in the later Poskim, and "whoever changes the wording which the Sages determined" makes the blessing a vain one (a *berakhah levatallah*). He suggests instead that *after* completing

the Shemoneh Esreh, when one steps back and recites
עושה השלום במרומיו, one should substitute עושה שלום במרומיו
for the usual עושה שלום במרומיו, for so he found in the
Arizal's diary. We see therefore that there were those
who viewed this change in the most serious light.

However, when we look into this further, we see that
what is involved here is not so much a *change* in the
wording as the *choice* of an alternative version for the Ten
Days of Repentance. Indeed, the phrase עושה השלום is
actually the usual conclusion of the Blessing עושה שלום according to the Eretz Israel version of the Shemoneh Esreh, and is preserved in Genizah fragments dating back
to Geonic times.[4] שים ש[לום על] ישראל עמך וברכינו ושמרינו [כולנו]
כאחד. כי טוב בעיניך לברך א[ת עמך] ישראל בשלום. בא״י עושה ה[שלום].
This version is also attested in midrashim from Eretz
Israel, as in Leviticus Rabba 9:9.[5]

> R. Mani of Sheab and R. Yehoshua of Sikhnin in the
> name of R. Levi: Great is peace, for all the good
> blessings and consolations which the Holy One,
> blessed be He, brought to Israel, conclude with
> "peace". In Keriat Shema: פורס סוכת שלום. In *Me'en*
> *HaBerachot*: מעין הברכות ועושה השלום.[6]

According to R. Menahem Mendel Landau, the author
of Emek Berakhah,

> It seems that in Babylonia they changed the conclu-
> sion of the Blessing of Peace to המברך את עמו ישראל
> בשלום, following the Talmud (Megillah 18a), which

based the wording on the verse ה׳ יברך את עמו בשלום
(Psalms 29:11). I have not found this version of the
berakhah anywhere but in Midrash Tanhuma (at the
beginning of Parashat Pinhas). The Ashkenazim in
early times held to the customs of Eretz Israel. . . .
Afterwards, when the customs embodied in the
Babylonian Talmud spread throughout Israel, they
did not wish to forgo their early customs, and so
they maintained them at specific times. Thus,
שאותך לבדך ביראה נעבוד for the Ten Days of Repentance, when other blessings' conclusions are also
changed, namely, המלך המשפט and המלך הקדוש. . . .
God forbid that we think that the Sages of
Ashkenaz created new versions of old *berakhot*.
Rather, all these versions date back to the days of
the Tannaim and Amoraim.

Thus, the alteration of עושה שלום to עושה השלום is one of
selection rather than actual change. They did not change
the wording, as the author of *Siddur ha-Shelah* thought,
but rather *they retained an earlier version* for the Ten Days
of Repentance.

We may assume that this ending was also known to
the Babylonian Geonim, for we find a report of a Geonic
responsum as follows.[7]

We found in one of the Geonic responsa that אלקינו
ואלוקי אבותינו ברכינו בברכה [המשולשת בתורה . . .] is not said
during Minhah, because the *kohanim* do not recite
their blessing at Minhah time, and therefore we do
not conclude [the Blessing of Peace with]

ישראל בשלום המברך את עמו. Likewise, when someone prays without a *minyan*, Birkat Kohanim is not said; Sim Shalom is recited with the conclusion עושה השלום.

However, there is no certainty that the entire passage is Geonic; from "therefore" onward may be a scribal addition.[8] The connection between this blessing and Birkat Kohanim is mentioned first in Megillah 18a.

> Why did they place Sim Shalom after Birkat Kohanim? As it is written: "And place My Name on the children of Israel and I will bless them" (Numbers 6:27). The blessing of the Holy One, blessed be He, is peace, as it is written: "God blesses His people Israel with peace" (Psalms 29:11).

It is little wonder that the "expounders of hints" and their like found hints in the number of words in this blessing. Thus, the *Kolbo* writes in Hilkhot Tefillah 11 (6a) that there are fifty-three words, corresponding to the fifty-three letters in the verse "May God raise His Face to you" (Numbers 6:26) and the following one, both from Birkat Kohanim. Thus, when there is no Birkat Kohanim this version is not needed, since the hint is unnecessary. And likewise, in the responsum cited above, when there is no Birkat Kohanim there are only fifty words, since the conclusion עושה השלום is three words shorter than the המברך את עמו ישראל בשלום. It may even be that the fifty-three words refers to the "short version" found in *Sefer ha-Manhig*, Dinei Tefillah, siman 66, ed. Rafael, p. 100, cited also in the *Beit Yosef*, O.H. 122, though it is rejected by both. Nevertheless, the version would have contained fifty-three words, concluding with עושה שלום ברכנו כלנו ברב עוז ושלום ברוך אתה ה׳ המברך את עמו בשלום.[9]

However, this remains speculative.

Notes

1. *Minhagei Yisrael*, vol. 2, pp. 178–181.
2. And Yom Kippur.
3. *Sefer ha-Maharil*, ed. R. Sh. Y. Spitzer (Jerusalem, 5749), p. 284.
4. See J. Mann, *Hebrew Union College Annual* 2 (1925): 307; see there p. 279, n. xviii.
5. Ed. Margulies, p. 194.
6. So in *Sefer Vehizhir*; see Margulies's notes on l. 5. The current text has עושה שלום. For other evidence, see Midrash Tehillim 29:2, ed. Buber, p. 232; Yalkut Samuel 1:2 in the name of Midrash Yelammedenu. So too, in Masekhet Soferim 10:6, ed. Higger, pp. 216–217. For evidence from the Rishonim, see Emek Berakhah in *Siddur Tzelota de-Avraham*, vol. 1, pp. 322–325, and additional notes in Sheruta di-Tzelota, p. 322. On מעין–מעון הברכות, see G. Alon, *Mehkarim be-Toldot Yisrael*, vol. 2 (1958), pp. 128-132.
7. See J. Mann, *Hebrew Union College Annual* 2 (1925): 317.
8. See Mann's comment, ibid., n. 107.
9. See the variant readings for l. 54 there, and note that we have slightly altered the version in the *Beit Yosef* by omitting two *vav*s.

PART VIII
YOM KIPPUR

CHAPTER 17[1]
Three Tevilot on Erev Yom Kippur

IT SHOULD BE CLEAR BY NOW that our Sages in all eras show a sensitivity to numerical matters which has become second nature in matters of *tefillah* and ritual. It is no wonder that symbolic numbers turn up in verses that in turn help shape customs and halakhot. Let us examine another application of this approach which will make this tendency even clearer.

The Tur in Orah Hayyim 606 writes:

> People are accustomed to immerse in the *mikveh* on the eve of Yom Kippur. Rav Amram Gaon said: "A

person should immerse during the seventh hour[2]
and [then] pray the Minhah prayer."[3] And Rav
Saadiah said: "When he rises from immersing, he
should make a blessing on the immersion," and my
father and teacher, the Rosh, ז״ל, wrote: "His opinion
does not seem reasonable to me, for we do not find
any mention of this immersion in the Talmud, nor
was it not established by the prophets. . . . And if
[this immersion is to fulfill] the [statement] of R.
Yitzhak, who said (Rosh Hashanah 16b): 'A person
is obligated to purify himself for the festival,' this
refers to purification from all impurities, even the
impurity caused by contact with a corpse, which
requires sprinkling on the third and seventh days
[and not merely immersion]. [Moreover,] these days
we have no purification.[4] And since those who have
had a seminal emission do not immerse during the
rest of the year [even though biblically this is
required], there is no obligation to immerse and
thus no blessing should be recited.[5] Nevertheless,
people have adopted the custom of purifying themselves for Yom Kippur of the impurity due to any
seminal emissions, and they rely on [a statement in]
Midrash Pirkei deR. Eliezer [chap. 46] that on Yom
Kippur they are as pure as the ministering angels.

In *Sefer Maharil* (p. 316) it is further written that the
Mahari Segal would immerse *three times,* both . . . on the
eve of Rosh Hashanah and the eve of Yom Kippur. The
same suggestion is made in the *Rokeah*,[6] the reason being
that the phrase מקוה ישראל ("the Hope of Israel," referring

to God, but here taken as "the Mikveh [ritualarium] of Is-rael") is mentioned three times in the Bible: Jeremiah 14:8 and 17:13, Ezra 10:2. *Sefer Hasidim* too has the same rule of three immersions, but derived from another expression and other verses: Women immerse three times because three verses speak of God's purification of Israel: Ezekiel 36:25, Leviticus 16:19 and 30 (see immediately below).[7] From this he concludes that whoever immerses on the eve of Yom Kippur must immerse three times as well.

The meaning of this seems to be that the word "puri-fy" appears three times in Ezekiel 36:22 and Leviticus 16:19 and 30 (three times when the two verses are com-bined); the latter verses deal with Yom Kippur specifi-cally. Thus the custom of immersing three times is also based on number symbolism.

Notes

1. *Minhagei Yisrael*, vol. 2, pp. 185–188.
2. The *BaH* explains that the seventh hour refers to a time before Minhah: "Since our Sages ruled that one should recite the Vidduy (Confession) during Minhah, before he eats and drinks [before Yom Kippur] . . . therefore we require that the prayer and confession be performed in purity. . . ." According to the *Beit Yosef*, the Tur's source is the Rosh on Yoma, chap. 8, siman 24. On the other hand, the Ram [= Maharam of Rothenberg] holds that one may immerse whenever he wants to, so long as it is before nightfall (*Tashbetz*, cited by the *Beit Yosef*; similarly, the *Kolbo*, siman 68, *Sefer ha-Minhagim de-Bei Maharam me-Routtenberg*, p. 53).

  Others (*Orhot Hayyim*, Hilkhot Yom ha-Kippurim) hold that Rav Amram Gaon ruled that the immersion should take place during the seventh or eighth hour, and that is the opinion to be found in our editions of *Seder Rav Amram Gaon*; on the other hand, the *Manhig* (Hilkhot Yom ha-Kippurim, siman 52, p. 341) writes in his name: "from six hours onward"; so too *Mahzor Vitry*, siman 343, p. 374; *Siddur Rashi*, siman 208, p. 95: six or eight hours; and in *Shibbolei ha-Leqet*, siman 310, p. 289: seven or eight hours; while *Tanya Rabbati*, siman 778: eight or nine. See R. Y. A. Zilber, *Berur Halakhah*, O.H. pt. 3 (Benei Brak, 5736), pp. 343–344 (to O.H. 606), and compare his comments on pp. 335–336 (to O.H. 581); and, finally, see the comments of the editor of *Sefer ha-Manhig*, ed. Rafael (Jerusalem, 5738), p. 341, to l. 71.

3. *Seder Rav Amram Gaon*, pt. II, siman 112, ed. Goldschmidt (Jerusalem, 5732), p. 160.

4. According to the Maharil, this immersion is because of the need *for repentance*, in order to facilitate one's entrance into the Day of Atonement; see ed. Spitzer, p. 315 (Hilkhot Yom Kippur, siman 3; and see Mishnah Yoma 3:3: No one may enter the Temple Court, even if he is ritually pure, until he has immersed himself). He cites an argument of Mahari Segal in defense of this position, since why then would everyone, including women and children, be required to immerse? Only men are subject to seminal emissions. If the argument be made that women too are subject to such emissions after marital congress, why then are virgins and old women required to immerse? The reason is certainly because of repentance. Thus, even if one immersed before Rosh Hashanah, and saw no seminal emission thereafter, he is required to immerse before Yom Kippur.

The source for this is the *Or Zarua*, vol. 1, siman 112, which connects repentance and immersion, based on Midrash Shoher Tov, mizmor 51, ed. Buber, p. 141a. See also *Minhagei Yisrael*, vol. 4, pp. 198–199, on the authority of customs that arose out of error.

5. See Maharil, siman 4, p. 387, where he cites another opinion, that the immersion is for purity, this based on Pirkei de-R. Eliezer, as the Tur writes below.

6. Siman 214 and 218, but not explicitly; see R. Spitzer's comment in his edition of the Maharil, n. 3.

7. Siman 394, ed. Margaliot, pp. 284–285.

PART IX
SUKKOT

CHAPTER 18[1]
Birkat ha-Haftarah on
Hol ha-Moed Sukkot

ACCORDING TO SHULHAN ARUKH, Orah Hayyim 663:2, "We conclude [the blessings after the Haftarah for Shabbat Hol ha-Moed Sukkot]: מקדש השבת וישראל והזמנים." The *BaH* wonders at this wording, since for Shabbat Hol ha-Moed Pesah the custom is to conclude with the words מקדש השבת.[2]

Goldschmidt discussed this problem, and concluded that the first to record this custom was the thirteenth-century halakhist, R. Hayyim Paltiel, a contemporary of the Maharam of Rothenburg.[3]

The custom is also found in the notes of his disciple, R. Avraham Klausner (fourteenth century),[4] and from there to the compilations of two of the latter's disciples, the Maharil[5] and R. Isaac Tyrnau.[6] However, as the annotator of R. Isaac Tyrnau's book already noted, this custom is found everywhere, and, he observed, it is necessary to explain why Sukkot differs from Pesah in this regard.

The Maharil, too, was bothered by this discrepancy, and recorded several reasons for it, suggested by Mahar Weibush. One possibility was that while Shabbat Hol ha-Moed Sukkot differs from the other days of Hol ha-Moed Sukkot in that two Torah scrolls are used, while only one is brought out on the other days, Shabbat Hol ha-Moed Pesah is no different from the other days of Hol ha-Moed Pesah—two scrolls are used each day. He also related this difference to the differences in the sacrifices offered on each day of Hol ha-Moed Sukkot, while all of Hol ha-Moed Pesah is uniform in this respect.

However, these reasons are problematic, as Goldschmidt already noted. What have the number of Torah scrolls or festival sacrifices to do with the *berakhot* of the Haftarah? Even though I do not have a complete solution to this problem, I do have some suggestive comments to make.

The source for this halakhah is to be found in Shabbat 24a: "R. Giddel said in the name of Rav: 'Whoever recites the Haftarah on Shabbat Rosh Hodesh need not mention Rosh Hodesh, for were it not for the Sabbath, there would be no Haftarah from the Prophets."[7] By the same token, we need not mention the festival on Shabbat Hol ha-Moed, as the Tashbetz and others decided.[8]

However, there are those who differ. The Ramban in *Sefer Milhamot* in Shabbat records the opinion of R. Y. Bargeloni: "Mar Rav Hai [Gaon] wrote that Rosh Hodesh should be mentioned by the one who recites the Haftarah on Shabbat Rosh Hodesh, and so is the custom." And, he comments, so have all the Geonim agreed.[9] And, we may add, so too the Baal ha-Maor and, interestingly, Rashi. In this case the Tosafists disagree with Rashi's custom! To these may be added the Rif, Rabbenu Hananel, the Rambam, *Siddur Rasag*,[10] *Seder Rav Amram Gaon*,[11] and Rabbenu Yonah.[12]

Why then did these authorities reject the statement of R. Giddel in the name of Rav? It would seem that this is because later in the sugya, after a number of other statements regarding the wording of various Haftarah *berakhot*, in the name of such Amoraim as R. Huna, R. Yehudah, and R. Ahdevoi, the sugya concludes that "the halakhah does not follow all these individual rules." Rashi, in his comments ad loc., includes the statement of R. Giddel within the list of rejected halakhot, as do the Rif, the Meiri, and the Rid.[13] However, Tosafot there observe that Rashi should not have included R. Giddel in the list, because custom follows his statement; so too Rabbenu Tam,[14] *Sefer ha-Terumah*,[15] and others.

Thus, the Geonim and Rishonim differ as to whether R. Giddel's statement on Rav's authority was included in *setama di-gemara*'s rejection of "all these rules." It may be that two of these different interpretations combined into one, contradictory custom. The one that rejected R. Giddel's rule, resulting in the custom of *mentioning* the festival on Shabbat Hol ha-Moed, was for some reason accepted in Ashkenaz for Sukkot. The other, which accepted his rule but applied it for Shabbat Hol ha-Moed Pesah, did *not* mention the festival.[16]

Notes

1. *Minhagei Yisrael*, vol. 1, pp. 125–127.
2. See also Rema, O.H. 490:9, and *Matteh Moshe*, siman 966–968, and the Magen Avraham there, n. 7, as well as 663:2.
3. See his *Mehqerei Tefillah u-Piyyut* (Jerusalem, 5739), pp. 395–396.
4. Ed. Y. Y. Dissen (Jerusalem, 5738), siman 59:3, p. 56. Compare siman 127:2, p. 120.
5. *Sefer Maharil*, p. 53b, ed. Spitzer, p. 380.
6. Ed. Spitzer, p. 135. See also p. 63, no. 27, n. 22.
7. This explanation is accepted by all the Amoraim, as Tosafot notes on Shabbat 24b, s.v. *ve-let hilkheta*, and so too the Rosh, siman 16. The decision appears in Shulhan Arukh, O.H. 284:2.
8. *Tashbetz* II:248, followed by Hida in *Birkei Yosef*, siman 425—we conclude with only מקדש השבת. So too the GRA, *Maaseh Rav*, siman 226; the Baal ha-Tanya in his Shulhan Arukh; and the custom in Jerusalem.
9. See *Otzar ha-Geonim*, Shabbat, Helek ha-Teshuvot, p. 26, siman 78, and see *Sefer ha-Itim*, p. 271.
10. P. 363.
11. II, end of siman 32, p. 276.
12. See *Enzykopedia Talmudit*, vol. 18, p. 30.

13. See the Meiri, p. 108, and *Piskei Rid*, ed. Wertheimer and Lis (Jerusalem, 5722), p. 236.
14. *Sefer ha-Yashar*, ed. Schlesinger, siman 216.
15. Siman 230.
16. For more on this, see the responsum of R. Yitzhak Nissim, ז״ל, which was published in *Sefer ha-Zikaron le-R. Yitzhak Nissim*, זצ״ל, ed. M. Benayahu, Helek Halakhah u-Minhag (Jerusalem, 5745), pp. 5–9.

CHAPTER 19[1]
Regarding the Crowns of the Torah Scrolls on Simhat Torat

AN INTERESTING CUSTOM from Geonic times is recorded in a responsum of R. Hai Gaon.[2] On Simhat Torah the Torah scrolls were adorned with special crowns, and these crowns were passed over the heads of those who received *aliyot* to the Torah.

> He was further asked: "In places where it is the custom to make a crown for each Torah scroll, whether of silver or gold, or of myrtle or from women's ornaments, such as bracelets, rings, and similar articles, and hang them on the crown and place [the crown] on the Torah scroll, either when it is within its covering or on [the covering itself] on the day of Simhat Torah, is it permissible to use women's ornaments [for this purpose]?"
>
> He replied: "Whether of one or the other, it is

permissible to place them on the Torah scroll . . . and to place [the crown] on the head of the reader [i.e., the one called for the *aliyah*]. . . . if it is considered proper in their eyes, let them do so, and there is no reason [to object]."[3]

We find the same custom mentioned in *Sefer ha-Manhig*.[4]

Regarding the wooden crown which [people] are accustomed to make on Simhat Torah, and which they cover with women's veils by sewing or weaving around them, and on which they place ornaments,[5] women's bracelets and their rings and other adornments, then placing the whole on the Torah scroll, and which at the time of the reading of the Torah they place on the head of the one who reads [= the one called for the *aliyah*] . . .

This custom is also mentioned by the Rashba, with the additional detail that the crown was placed on children as well; the Rashba responded to the inquiry by suggesting that it would be well to refrain from this practice, although "I have heard that this custom has spread to most places among Jews, and I have never heard of anyone protesting."[6]

This custom was accompanied by other, similar celebratory practices, such as reciting praises of Torah and thanking God for giving it to us. R. Yitzhak Gi'at mentions that along with the praises there was a custom to bring *mugmarot*, incenselike spices which added to the atmosphere of thanksgiving and celebration. He also mentions other *hiddurin*—adornments, ornamentations, or embellishments. Could these *hiddurin* be the crowns made for the Torah scroll?

Additional evidence for the ancient custom of adorning the completion of a cycle of Torah study may be gleaned from the Hadran recited after one has studied a tractate of Talmud. The word *hadran* has been the focus of much discussion. *Sefer Eshkol* quotes the Raavad, who connected it with the Aramaic *h-d-r*, the equivalent of the Hebrew *h-z-r*, "to return" and thus "to repeat, to review." Since reviewing the tractate just completed is the surest way of retaining one's knowledge of it, Raavad connects the word with this root.[7] The sixteenth-century grammarian R. Elijah Bahur, however, expressed his doubt as to the function of the *nun*,[8] since the form *hadarna* would be expected, and other explanations have been suggested.

R. Hayyim b. Bezalel, the brother of the Maharal of Prague, in his work *Sefer ha-Hayyim*,[9] connected the form with the noun *hadar*, "glory." The word would then mean "our glory." He explained that "since the Talmud is glorious only when studied by Jews, and Israel itself is distinguished precisely by its adherence to the Oral Torah, which separates it from the nations, we therefore are accustomed to declare at the completion of a tractate that 'our glory is on you, and your glory is on us.'"[10]

R. Reuven Margaliot suggested that this formula

goes back to the Temple service. In support of this contention he cites two Talmudic passages. One is Rosh Hashanah 31b, where R. Anan b. Rava, in the name of Rav, relates that at the conclusion of the Sabbath Musaf sacrifices they would say: "*Ziv* [Glory] is yours."[11] The second is Sukkah 45a, relating to Mishnah Sukkah 4:5: "At the time of their leaving what would they say? 'Beauty is yours, O altar, beauty is yours, O altar.'"

Rav Margaliot thus suggests that the phrase "Glory and beauty is yours, O altar" would be recited at the conclusion of the service, and this is what is referred to by the expression *hadrakh*, "your glory."

In the light of all this, it is possible that the custom of adorning the Torah scroll with a crown, and of placing this crown on the heads of those going up for an *aliyah*, was a way of concretizing the concept alluded to upon completing a chapter of the Oral Torah: "Your glory is on us, and our glory on you."

Additional proof for this suggestion may be found in a passage in *Aqedat Yitzhak* of R. Yitzhak Arama, Devarim, Gate 87, where he records an alternative reading of the Hadran: *hadrakh alan ve-hadran alakh, zivakh alan ve-zivan alakh.*[12]

Notes

1. *Minhagei Yisrael*, vol. 1, pp. 128–131.
2. *Shaarei Simhah* of R. Yitzhak Gi'at, pt. I, 117:8.
3. See also *Otzar ha-Geonim* to Megillah, siman 177, p. 51, and see the Zohar III, p. 256b.
4. "Yom Shemini ve-Inyan Simhat Torah," siman 59, ed.

Rafael, II, pp. 417–418.

5. Proverbs 25:12.

6. *Teshuvot ha-Rashba ha-Meyuhasot le-Ramban,* siman 260.

7. See *Sefer Eshkol,* ed. Auerbach, pp. 49–50; ed. Albeck, p. 160.

8. *Sefer ha-Tishbi,* s.v. *hadar.*

9. (Cracow, 5353), Zekhuyot, chap. 3.

10. See R. R. Margaliot, *Olelot* (Jerusalem, 5707), pp. 11–12.

11. So too, in Yerushalmi Megillah 3:7.

12. See also R. Tuviah Preschel, *Sinai* 96, 3–4 (5745): 585–586.

CHAPTER 20[1]
The Hadar in the Hadran

IN THE PRECEDING CHAPTER I discussed the recitation of the Hadran on the completion of a portion of the Oral Torah, and tried to connect it with the custom of adorning the Torah scroll with a crown on Simhat Torah. An essential part of my argument is the difficulty of interpreting the word *hadran* as meaning (in Aramaic) "we have reviewed," because of the lack of a final *alef*: *hadarna* or *hadrana*. However, in early Geonic sources this *alef* does appear. In Manuscript C of Bava Metzia, described by Prof. Shamma Friedman, at the end of each chapter we find: הדרנא עלך איזה הוא נשך, הדרנא עלך השוכר את האומנין, the meaning being, apparently, either "We have completed reading you,"[2] or, perhaps, "We have reviewed you."[3]

However, in complete manuscripts the usual spelling is without the final *alef*,[4] and, as I noted above, can easily be explained according to the suggestion of the

187

Maharal's brother, R. Hayyim b. Bezalel, as connected with the word *hadar*, "glory." The alternative is nevertheless possible; even without the final *nun*, the word הדרן can be taken as a short form of הדרנא, just as אמרנא = אמרנו = אמרן, or, as in the Jewish Aramaic documents from Elephantine in southern Egypt, which date to the early Second Temple Persian period, אנחן = אנחנא = אנחנו. This form is also known from the Babylonian Talmud, as in Bava Batra 73b, "when we return after twelve months of the year," with the spelling הדרן, and elsewhere. It seems that this form still existed in Geonic times.[5]

It is thus possible that while the original form was הדרנא עלך, with the meaning "We have reviewed you," later, in the Geonic period, when the form הדרן became common, an element of ambiguity entered in, and the word could be interpreted as "our glory" as well as "we reviewed." This is especially the case in the context of the second phrase, הדרן עלך, which can only be interpreted as a noun, and not as a verb.[6]

This double-meaning is revealed to us in a responsum of R. Mattaniah Gaon, where the two words occur in tandem: "Even though it is permitted to bake matzah on the eve of Shabbat, they went back (חזרו) and adorned (הדרו) the mitzvah by baking [the matzah] after Shabbat, in its time."[7] The same double-meaning may occur in the Hadran.[8]

Notes
1. *Minhagei Yisrael*, vol. 1, pp. 132–134.
2. See Ketubot 77b: "Leave me for thirty days, until I com-

plete my learning (עד דנהדר לתלמודאי)." See *Diqduqei Soferim ha-Shalem*, p. 222, l. 32, and compare Moed Qatan 28a, Ketubot 38b, Hulin 86b, Keritot 27a.

3. See *Alei Sefer* 9 (5641): 13.

4. Ibid., n. 12. See Y. Sussman's note in his "Masoret Limmud u-Masoret Nusah shel ha-Talmud ha-Yerushalmi: Leverur Nushaoteha shel Yerushalmi Masekhet Sheqalim," *Mehqarim be-Sifrut ha-Talmudit . . . le-Shaul Lieberman . . .* (Jerusalem, 5743), pp. 32–33.

5. My friend and colleague, Prof. Shamma Friedman, has noted that this form appears in early Aramaic inscriptions; see J. Gibson, *Textbook of Syrian Inscriptions*, vol. 2 Oxford, 1975), p. 43, and there are Syriac parallels as well, and perhaps in Mandaic. In early manuscripts of the Talmud, the essential form is אמרנה, with the variant אמרין. In later manuscripts the forms אמרן—הדרן appear; for some reason this early form reappears in later texts alongside the later forms. R. Y. N. Epstein, *Diqduq Aramit Bavlit* (Tel Aviv–Jerusalem, 1960), pp. 35–36, considers הדרן to be the primary form; so too Y. Kutscher, *Mehqarim be-Ivrit uve-Aramit* (Jerusalem, 5737), p. 243, but see Friedman's objections in *Alei Sefer* 9, p. 31.

6. My thanks to Prof. Friedman for his enlightening comments on this matter.

7. *Shaarei Teshuvah*, siman 294, and in a shortened form, siman 93; *Ittur* II, p. 122. See *Otzar ha-Geonim* to Pesahim, p. 65. See also Tur, O.H. 458, where the form is חזקו, "they strengthened," in place of חזרו, and compare the responsum of R. Yehudai Gaon in *Mahzor Vitry*, siman 23, p. 261; *Mordekhai*, Pesahim, siman 543; *Otzar ha-Geonim* to Pesahim, p. 66, where yet another possibility appears: הזהרו. See also Y. Gartner, *Sinai* 82 (5738), and esp. pp. 122–128.

8. On the use of one word in two senses, see the excellent article by D. Boyarin in *Eshel Be'er Sheva* 3 (5746): 91–99; and see D. Sadan, *Galgal ha-Moadim–Shabbat ve-Shalosh Regalim* (Tel Aviv, 1964), pp. 169 f.

CHAPTER 21[1]
Hatan ha-Torah—Hatam Torah

ABRAHAM YAARI, in his monumental work, *Toledot Hag Simhat Torah* (Jerusalem, 5724), pp. 66–67, suggested that the original form of the term חתן תורה, the title of the last *aliyah* to the Torah on Simhat Torah, was originally חתם תורה, literally, "the sealing [completion] of the Torah," which, through a natural linguistic process became חתן תורה, "bridegroom of the Torah," especially in the context of the great joy which accompanies the Torah reading on that day.

As Yaari notes, this is not mere speculation, since we have evidence that the *aliyah* was called חתם תורה in the sixteenth century. R. Yisachar Ibn Susan, a North African scholar who settled in Safed and recorded the customs of many communities, writes: "After that the fifth [person] goes up [for an *aliyah*], and he is the one who completes [the reading] . . . in order to complete (לחתום) the

191

Torah, and he is called חתם תורה."[2]

In the communities of Comtat-Venaissin in south-eastern France —Avignon, Carpentras, L'Isle sur la Sorgue, Cavaillon—the one receiving this *aliyah* was also called the חותם תורה.

If Yaari is correct, and the original term for this *aliyah* was חתם תורה, and it is not the result of a later "correction," we may add yet another explanation to the name. In the time of Hazal in Eretz Israel, we find that final *mem*s were often pronounced as *nun*s. Thus, for example, in some early manuscripts the word אדם, "man," is written אדן.[3] Other examples are כרן = כרם (Mishnah Bava Batra 4:9 in the Kaufman manuscript), שלון = שלום, and דרון = דרום. A number of scholars have noted that this phenomenon is known as late as the time of the Ramban.[4] If so, it is possible that the term חתן תורה is an Eretz Israel form of חתם תורה, and that חתן = חתם. חתם תורה is thus the original form, especially since the "crowns" associated with the חתמים brought to mind those associated with weddings; according to Mishnah Sotah 9:14, after the destruction of the Temple, the crowns which brides wore were banned. (See above, Chapter 19.)

Proof for this lies in the provenance of the term. Yaari shows that the term חתן first appears in France in the works of Rashi's students, in *Siddur Rashi* and *Mahzor Vitry*.[5] We also find it in Germany, as in *Sefer Roqe'ah*.[6] This is in line with the known influence of Eretz Israel customs on Franco-German Jewry. It may be, however, that once the term reached France and Germany, it was understood as referring to a "bridgegroom." This would explain why *Mahzor Vitry* goes out of its way to explain the link between חתן תורה and a bridegroom at a wedding: וגם הוא חתן נעלה כמחנך ונכנס לחופה, "and he [= the חתם בראשית]) *also* [may be considered] an elevated bridegroom, as one who inaugurates and enters into the *huppah*."

Notes

1. *Minhagei Yisrael,* vol. 1, pp. 135–137, and vol. 2, p. 274.
2. Later on he records an alternative designation: "Some call him חתן תורה." His book is called *Ibbur Shanim,* later changed to *Tiqqun Yisachar,* by R. Yisachar b. R. Mordekhai Ibn Susan (Constantinople, 5324), II, Minhagot, s.v. Simhat Torah [unpaginated]. See further Y.B. Wilhelm, *Tarbiz* 44, 1956, p. 132; A. Leshem, *Shabbat u-Moadei Yisrael* 2, (1969), p. 536; and also R. Eliyahu Halevy, *Responsa Zekan Aharon* (Constantinople 1734), Siman 206. (He died c. 1540.)
3. See Y. N. Epstein in his *Mavo le-Nusah ha-Mishnah,* pp. 1230–1232, where a number of examples are cited.
4. See S. Asaf, *Sifran shel Rishonim,* p. 94.
5. See Yaari, *Toledot Hag Simhat Torah,* p. 64, and see *Siddur Rashi,* siman 308, p. 148, and *Mahzor Vitry,* p. 408.
6. Siman 284, p. 126.

CHAPTER 22[1]
The Haftarah of Simhat Torah

THE WHOLE ISSUE OF THE HAFTARAH for Simhat Torah and
its development is discussed in great detail in Avraham
Yaari's work, *Toledot HAG Simhat Torah*.[2]

Here I wish to add several pertinent comments.

There are a number of customs regarding the Haftarah for Simhat Torah which were prevalent in various
parts of France and Spain in time of the Rishonim. Basic-
ally, the Haftarah was taken from either I Kings 8:22–53
(King Solomon's dedication of the Temple) or Joshua 1
(the accession of Joshua to the leadership of Israel after
Moses' death), or from combinations of the two.

Thus, *Sefer Eshkol* of R. Avraham b. R. Yitzhak of
Narbonne (first half of the twelfth century) records the
custom of reciting the I Kings passage, in accordance
with the Bavli Megillah 31a. But, he adds:

It has become the custom (אבל נהגו) to recite the Haftarah of Joshua 1, in accordance with the Yerushalmi. However, since [that chapter] ends with Moses'
death, it is proper to add something from the continuation, and the custom has arisen of reciting the
first eight verses of Joshua and continuing with I
King 8:22. It is proper to take both—do not neglect
this.[3]

Sefer ha-Makhkim, by R. Nathan b. R. Yehudah, a
Provençal scholar two centuries after the author of the
Eshkol, records a variation of this custom, in which only
three verses from Joshua are recited before moving on to
I Kings.[4]

On the other hand, *Sefer Orhot Hayyim*, by R. Aaron
ha-Kohen of Lunel, a Provençal contemporary of the
author of *Sefer ha-Makhkim*, records two entirely different
customs, both based exclusively on what *Sefer ha-Eshkol*
considers "Yerushalmi": reciting all of Joshua 1, and, as
"in all the districts of Catalonia," concluding with
"wherever you go" (v. 9). The Abudarham, whose fourteenth-century Spanish work on prayer has become
authoritative, records a custom identical to the "Cata-
lonian" one cited by *Orhot Hayyim*.

Yet another variation is to be found in *Sefer
ha-Manhig*: "Some conclude with 'After the death of
Moses,' and it seems proper to conclude with I Kings
8."[5]

Finally, a Yemenite custom is to recite the first nine
verses of Joshua and then the last verse of chapter 6[6]—

ten verses in all, according to the Rambam's opinion in Seder Haftarot in Sefer Ahavah.

Thus, we have a range of variation in regard to the Haftarah from Joshua; some read three verses, some eight, some nine, some ten, and some recite the entire chapter, which contains eighteen. Why this great variation? Moreover, all of these practices reject the Bavli's recommendation of I Kings 8:22–53, a fact which also requires explanation.[7]

In order to understand this confusing welter of customs, we must remember that the foundation of the recitation of the Haftarah is the requirement to read a passage from the Prophets that is relevant to the Torah reading and resembles it in form[8]—i.e., in regard to the number of verses it contains. It is for this reason that a *baraita* cited in both Talmuds (Bavli Megillah 23a and Yerushalmi Megillah 4:2) requires that not less than twenty-one verses be recited—three corresponding to each *aliyah*, 7 x 3 = 21.[9] Likewise, the one reciting the Haftarah recites seven *berakhot* on the Sabbath. On festivals, when only five are called up to the Torah, fifteen verses are sufficient—5 x 3 = 15.[10]

Thus, since we are dealing with a festival Haftarah, there is no need for twenty-one verses, and the first chapter of Joshua, which contains eighteen verses, would be sufficient.[11] For this reason it seems that the custom of reading the first chapter of Joshua involved reading *only* that and nothing else, since it contains a sufficient number of verses, with no need to add verses from I Kings 8. And this is the custom referred to by Rav Amram Gaon.[12]

However, the essential question remains: why did the communities which adopted these customs depart from the Talmud's prescription of I Kings 8? The answer seems to be that they adopted the custom referred to in a Yerushalmi, as *Sefer Eshkol* mentions. Indeed, *Sefer Ravyah* quotes this passage from the Yerushalmi: "But in the Exile they read [the sidra of] Vezot Haberakhah on the ninth [day of the Sukkot–Shemini Atzeret festival] and recite the Haftarah of 'After the death of Moses.'"[13] The Rosh too refers to this Yerushalmi,[14] as does the Tur,[15] and from there to *Shiltei ha-Gibborim* on the Rif Megillah 11a (Rif pagination).[16]

Unfortunately, we do not have this passage in our copies of the Yerushalmi, but it seems likely that the citation comes from the *"Sefer Yerushalmi"* mentioned by the Rishonim—i.e., a work originating in Eretz Israel.[17] It seems therefore that we have here yet another example of different customs in Babylonia and Eretz Israel, with some communities choosing one, others choosing the other, and yet others combining them in various ways.

Understandably, for those who followed the Bavli and read the passage from I Kings, there was really no need to add very much from the passage in Joshua, since the Kings passage contains thirty-one verses.[18] Thus we have the custom of only reading three verses from the book of Joshua, either because the correspondence between the Torah reading and the Haftarah involves

only three verses,[19] according to the Bavli, or because
the entire Haftarah may consist of only three verses, according to the Yerushalmi,[20] at least when a *meturgeman*
was present to translate the Torah reading into Aramaic,
or to deliver a sermon. According to Masekhet Soferim,
three, five, or seven verses were enough.[21]

As for the custom of reading eight verses, noted
above, there seem to be two reasons here as well: either
because the eight verses added to the end of the book of
Deuteronomy (34:5–12) by Joshua, at least according to
R. Yehudah or R. Nehemiah in Bava Batra 15a, constitute
a *parashah* added to a Torah reading,[22] or because most
Haftarot consisted of eight verses, as appears from the
various Genizah fragments, corresponding to the number of *olim* including the Maftir.[23] Thus the custom of
reading eight verses from the first chapter of Joshua as a
Haftarah for Simhat Torah seems to have come from an
Eretz Israel background.

However, reading eight verses brought another
problem in its wake. According to the Talmud, the reading should be chosen so as not to leave less than three
verses until the end of the masoretic *parashah*, or paragraph.[24] In the case of Joshua 1, there is a break at the
end of verse 9, and reading only the first eight verses
violates the rule. It seems that this was the reason that
some communities added verse 9 to the Haftarah, thus
making a nine-verse reading.

Finally, the Yemenite custom, based on the Rambam,
which adds Joshua 6:27 to Joshua 1:1–9, making a total

of ten verses in all, is based on a Bavli which cites a custom of Eretz Israel. R. Shmuel b. Abba reports that he observed R. Yohanan's surprise when ten verses were read in the Haftarah; the *Gemara* replies that when there is a *meturgeman* this is permitted.[25] Likewise, R. Yohanan is reported to have said that a Haftarah cannot be less than ten verses, corresponding to the Ten Sayings with which the world was created.

The skip to Joshua 6 from Joshua 1 seems to have been made in order to fit the Haftarah to the Torah reading, for both Deuteronomy 34:9 and Joshua 6:27 speak of Joshua's close relationship to God. Deuteronomy reports that "Joshua bin Nun was full of the spirit of wisdom, for Moses had placed his hand on him, and all Israel listened to him, and did all God had commanded Moses," while the verse in Joshua says that "God was with Joshua, and his reputation spread throughout the land."[26]

In short, then, nearly all of the various customs regarding the exact reading of the Haftarah for Simhat Torah involve views originating in Eretz Israel.

Notes

1. *Minhagei Yisrael*, vol. 1, pp. 154–161.
2. Fifth chapter.
3. Ed. Auerbach, II, siman 21, p. 65.
4. Ed. Freimann, published in *Haeshkol* 6 (Cracow, 5669): 158. See Yaari, p. 58. This custom follows the opinion of R. Yehudai Gaon cited in *Siddur Rashi*, siman 308, pp. 148–149 and *Mahzor Vitry*, siman 418, p. 459.
5. Ed. Rafael, siman 56, pp. 415–416, and see the editor's notes.

6. Yaari, p. 59, in the name of R. Yosef Kafih.

7. N. Wieder, in an article in *Sefer Asaf*, pp. 257–258, suggests that the reading we have in the Bavli is not certain, since the Munich manuscript adds the I Kings passage to Megillah 31a. It seems to me, however, that a later scribe added this in accordance with his own custom.

8. See H. Luban in *Sinai* 70 (1972): 127–128.

9. However, there seems to have been a custom which required twenty-two verses, adding one for the *hazzan ha-kenesset*; see Masekhet Soferim 13:15, ed. Higger (New York, 5697), p. 271, n. 142. Indeed, we find several *haftarot* which do contain twenty-two verses, as in the Ashkenazic Haftarah for Parashat Shemot, which, with the addition of two verses, is twenty-two verses long, and the Haftarah of Yitro. See the Yeshiva University dissertation of M. Luban, "The Triennial Cycle" (1973), pp. 60–62, esp. n. 41.

10. See Responsa Maharam Padua, siman 78, and see Shulhan Arukh, O.H. 284:1.

11. And certainly if the subject of the Haftarah is concluded in less than twenty-one verses on Shabbat, there is no need to artificially lengthen the Haftarah. Thus we have the Haftarah of Tzav, which contains nineteen verses (Megillah 23b).

12. Ed. Goldschmidt, p. 177.

13. Siman 595; see the notes by the editor.

14. Megillah 4, siman 10.

15. O.H. 669.

16. Siman 2.

17. I hope to deal with this *Sefer* on another occasion.

18. In regard to the question of the author of *Tiqqun Yissachar*, that ordinarily one is not permitted to skip from one book of the Prophets to another, cited by Yaari, p. 58, see *Enzyclopedia Talmudit*, vol. 10, s.v. *haftarah*, p. 9, nn. 157–159, in the name of the *Terumat ha-Deshen*.

19. See Bavli Megillah 21b–22a.
20. See Luban's dissertation (n. 9 above), pp. 55–60. However, it seems that at times only *two* verses were read; see E. Z. Melammed in *Tarbiz* 24 (5715): 75.
21. Megillah 4:3 (p. 75c), and see Masekhet Soferim 13:15, ed. Higger, p. 250.
22. See S. H. Kook, *Iyyunim u-Mehqarim*, vol. 2, p. 42, and Rashi on Bava Batra 15a or Ri Migash, cited in *Shittah Mequbetzet* there.
23. See N. Fried, *Textus* 6 (1968): 121, esp. n. 19.
24. Megillah 21b–22a.
25. Megillah 23a.
26. Luban, diss., p. 62.

PART X
HANNUKAH

CHAPTER 23[1]
הנרות הללו קודש הם

IN ONE OF HIS RESPONSA the Maharshal writes that the
proper version of Hanerot Halalu recited after kindling
the Hannukah lights is as follows:

> הנרות הללו אנו מדליקין על התשועות ועל הנסים ועל הנפלאות
> שעשית לאבותינו על ידי כהניך הקדושים. וכל שמונת ימי חנוכה
> הנרות הללו קודש הם ואין לנו רשות להשתמש בהם אלא לראותם
> בלבד. כדי להודות לשמך על נפלאותיך ועל נסיך ועל ישועתך.

These lights we kindle for the salvations, for the
miracles, and for the wonders which You performed for our ancestors through Your holy priests.

And all eight days of Hannukah these lights are holy, and we have no right to make use of them but only to view them in order to give thanks to Your Name for Your wonders and for Your miracles and for Your salvations.

And, he adds, "Nothing should be changed or deleted. The reason for this is clear: It corresponds to the number thirty-six, aside from the opening words, 'these lights,' as though to say: 'these candles are thirty-six.' "[2] Thus, the thirty-six words correspond to the thirty-six lights which are kindled during the eight days of Hannukah.

This version of the recitation appears in the Tur as well, with the additional comment that "this was the custom of R. Meir of Rothenburg and my master and father, the Rosh, z.l."[3]

This prayer is taken from Masekhet Soferim 20:4, as a number of Rishonim note.[4]

Daniel Goldschmidt dealt with this prayer in a penetrating article.[5] In it, he noted that the custom of reciting it is not mentioned in the codes of the Rif and the Rambam, nor in works issuing from Rashi's school, nor even in the *Or Zarua* or the *Roqe'ah*.

Acceptance of this custom (as well as the acceptance of this particular version) may be tied to one man only, whose authority and influence on the religion of the Jews of Germany in the Middle Ages and on their customs was particularly strong; that man was R. Meir b. R. Barukh (Maharam) of Rothenburg, who lived in Germany in the thirteenth century.[6]

However, Goldschmidt did not deal with one puzzling issue connected with the version of Hanerot Halalu cited by the Maharshal—this version does not contain thirty-six words, or even thirty-eight (including the first two words), but forty-one! Among the Aharonim who dealt with this problem is the author of *Matteh Moshe*.[7] He solves the problem by noting that in the printed siddur of his teacher, the Maharshal, there is no *al* before *ha-nisim*, thus yielding thirty-six words when the opening הנרות הללו אנו מדליקין is not counted.[8] The same problem is discussed in *Elya Rabbah*,[9] but the author suggests deleting the word הן.

All these suggestions do not solve the problem of the version cited in the Rosh,[10] which contains, as *Matteh Moshe* notes, no less than *forty-four* words. When we look at the version which the Maharam himself cites in a responsum, we find thirty-eight, which, not counting the opening two words, yields the thirty-six that Maharam requires.

> הנרות הללו אנו מדליקין על התשועות ועל הנסים ועל הנפלאות
> שעשית לאבותינו על ידי כהניך הקדושים. (וכל) שמונת ימי חנוכה
> הנרות הללו קודש הן ואין לנו רשות להשתמש בהם אלא לראותם
> בלבד. להודות לשמך על נפלאותיך ועל נסיך ועל ישועתך.

Thus, while the Maharshal cited the proper number as given by the Maharam, he quoted his own version of the actual prayer, while the Maharam's version does not correspond to our text of Masekhet Soferim.

As noted, the custom of reciting Hanerot Halalu is

not mentioned either in the Bavli or the Yerushalmi, or even in Geonic literature. The question thus arises: Why did the Maharam insist on its obligatory nature?

The reason may be halakhic. Shulhan Arukh, O.H. 673:1, cites the Tur on the prohibition of using the light of the Hannukah lamps for any purpose whatsoever, even for religious purposes, according to some.

> It is forbidden to make use of the Hannukah lamp, whether on Shabbat or during the week; it is forbidden even to examine coins or count them by its light. [This applies as well] to holy purposes, such as studying Torah by its light; this [too] is forbidden. However, some permit a holy purpose.

Apparently most Poskim forbid the latter, but the Sages of Provence, in particular the Baal Ha-Ittur[11] and the Baal HaMaor,[12] did permit such use in the thirteenth century. It is possible, then, that the Maharam in the next century, in order to make it abundantly clear that such use was forbidden, chose to introduce the Hanerot Halalu, which he knew from an ancient Eretz Israel source, Masekhet Soferim.

It seems that the reason for the prohibition of the use of the Hannukah lights even for religious purposes must be assumed to stem from an *issur qedushah*, and not merely an *issur hana'ah* which is intended to prevent their use in a demeaning way (*bizayon*). As the Meiri to Shabbat 21a notes: "Some attribute this to an *issur hana'ah* and complete *qedushah* (קדושה גמורה); since they are a remembrance of the lamps and oil in the Temple, they set aside its use entirely for [purposes of the mitzvah]."[13]

For this reason the Poskim also prohibited the oil remaining in the lamps after the requisite time for lighting passes; among them are the Abudarham,[14] *Sefer Eshkol*,[15] and *Hiddushei ha-Rashba*.[16]

> HaRav Alfasi, ז״ל, in the Halakhot, explained that if the lamp was burning to this measure, and [the one who lit it] wishes to put it out, or to make use of its light, he may do so. . . . But some of the Geonim, ז״ל, said that if the lamp went out, and oil was left in it on the first day, he may add to it and kindle it on the second, and so too the other days. If some is left over on the last day, he must make a bonfire and burn it in its place, for it has become set aside (*huqtzah*) for the purposes of its mitzvah [and nothing else].

This view of "some of the Geonim" is the view of the *She'iltot*[17] and appears in the Pesikta Rabbati nearly word for word,[18] as well as in Midrash Tanhuma.[19]

However, the halakhah was not decided in accordance with this view, as the Rema noted: "All of this is so long as [the lamps] are burning for their mitzvah, but after their mitzvah [has been accomplished], they are permitted for [personal] use, and it is certainly permitted to light [other lamps] from them."[20]

Echoes of the other view appear in the customs of some other communities. The Jews of Kurdistan, according to A. Brauer in his book on them,[21] follow the custom of gathering the remainder of the oil and wicks used on Hannukah and making a bonfire, around which men dance at the conclusion of Hannukah. A similar custom may be found in Worms, where, according to R. Juspa Shammash, in his work, *Minhagim di-Qehala Qadisha Vermaiza*,[22] "that which remains on the eighth day is forbidden for benefit, and on the day of the *hannukah* of the altar [= the eighth day of Hannukah] one makes a bonfire and burns the remainder of the candles, in order that people should not inadvertently violate the prohibition."

Before leaving the subject of Hannukah, it is worth investigating the reason for the common use of wax candles in Eastern Europe and, to a great extent, in America, despite the Rema's clear preference for olive oil lamps.

It is laid down in the Shulhan Arukh as follows:

All oils and wicks are *kasher* for [use as] a Hannukah light, even if the oil [used] does not well into the wicks, and the flame does not catch well onto the wicks.

On this Rema comments:

However, [the use of] olive oil [will furnish] the most excellent mitzvah (*mitzvah min ha-muvhar*) (*Mordekhai*, *Kolbo*, and Maharil),[23] but if there is no olive oil [available], it is a mitzvah [to use] oil whose light is clean and pure, *and in these districts the custom is to light with wax candles*, for their light is as clear as that of oil.

This too was the custom of the Maharshal, as we learn from his responsa (siman 85):

> Olive oil [furnishes] a most excellent mitzvah, but if there is no olive oil available, let him take other oils. But, as regards animal fats (*shomen ve-helev*), it seems most likely that there is a greater *hiddur mitzvah* [more] *in [using] wax, and this is the custom.*

So too, the *Levush*.

Thus, a survey of Ashkenazic halakhic sources demonstrates that wax candles were used most, despite the fact that olive oil was considered a *mitzvah min ha-muvhar* and even though the Maharam of Rothenburg used oil.[24] It seems that this was the case because of the high price of olive oil in those parts of Europe, much higher than other oils or wax, as is explicitly mentioned in *Sefer Maharil* (MS Vienna 77, written in Italy in the year 5230 [= 1470]:[25] "Olive oil is the most expensive oil in the districts of the Rhine.").[26]

However, there is another factor to be taken into account. R. Yitzhak Yosef, in his collection of the opinions of his father, R. Ovadiah Yosef, *Yalqut Yosef*,[27] notes a strange paradox, already remarked upon by the *TaZ*. Though Sephardim in general, and R. Yosef Karo in particular, follow the views of the Rambam, and Ashkenazim those of Tosafot, custom has in this case reversed the usual trend. Rambam holds that the mitzvah of kindling Hannukah lights falls on each member of the household,[28] while Tosafot hold that even if the household is large, only one lamp should be lit—no more than eight lights on the last day of Hannukah.[29] In stark contrast with their usual practice, Ashkenazim follow the Rambam, while Sephardim follow Tosafot. In any case, as for the question of whether to use wax candles or olive oil, if olive oil was the most expensive of all, imagine how much more the cost would have been according to the Ashkenazic custom that each member of a household kindle his or her own olive-oil lamp![30]

An intermediate position was suggested in *Responsa Shevut Yaakov*: using olive oil for the first lamp each night, and using other, cheaper oils for the remaining lights.[31] As further evidence for the expense of using olive oil, my dear son, David, שי״ל, referred me to the words of the *Shelah*:[32] "It is a *mitzvah min ha-muvhar* to try to obtain oil rather than wax candles (*kandlie*), *even to buy it at a high price* . . . , and in particular, olive oil."

In order to verify the high price of olive oil in Poland in the time of the Rema, I turned to my colleague Prof. Moshe Rosman, of the Bar-Ilan History Department, who is an authority on Polish history. He referred me to the work of Julian Pelc, *Ceny w Krakovie w Latach 1369–1600* ("Prices in Cracow, 1369–1600"), published in Lwow in 1935, which includes the time of the Rema, who lived from 1525 to 1572. According to Pelc, a *kamien* of olive oil cost 160 groshen in the middle of the sixteenth century. Indeed, prices for olive oil rose in these years, from 88 in 1547 to 90 in 1548, to 120 in 1559 and 172.20 in 1583, perhaps doubling in the Rema's lifetime.

Moreover, since these are wholesale prices, the cost to consumers was still higher. It is impossible to ascertain what the price was in winter, at Hannukah time, but it was presumably still higher, since transportation in winter was difficult.

Unfortunately, wax was only about ten-percent cheaper, and it is doubtful that a *mitzvah min ha-muvhar* would have been put aside for such a small savings. It may be, therefore, that "wax" refers to tallow, which was about *one-quarter* the price of olive oil (see Pelc, pp. 37–38); it may be that *sha'avah* at times refers to tallow candles rather than those of wax. If so, the savings would be much more meaningful.[33]

As for the halakhic question of using tallow candles for Hannukah lamps, see the long discussion in *Sedei Hemed*, vol. 9, pp. 101b f., n. 17.

Notes

1. *Minhagei Yisrael*, vol. 1, pp. 162–166, and vol. 4, pp. 68–70.
2. *Shut Maharshal*, siman 85.
3. Tur, O.H. 676. So too in the *Mordekhai*, Shabbat, siman 268, in the gloss, *Hagahot Maimoniyot* on Hilkhot Hannukah 3, siman 1, with slight differences. See also the Aburdarham on *Seder Hadlaqat Ner Hannukah*, who explains the correspondence and the origin of the prayer.
4. See ed. Higger, pp. 343–344.
5. Now included in his *Mehqerei Tefillah u-Piyyut*, pp. 399–402.
6. Ibid., p. 400.
7. Siman 981.
8. Deleting one על and the four opening words yields 41 - 5 = 36.

9. 676:4–5.
10. Rosh, Shabbat, chap. 3, end of siman 8.
11. Hilkhot Hannukah, p. 115a, cited in *Shibbolei ha-Leqet*, siman 165, p. 72a, and in *Kolbo*, siman 44.
12. See *Ha-Ma'or ha-Qatan*, "Bameh Madliqin," 9a, s.v. *le-man de-amar*.
13. The placement of the Hannukah menorah in the southern part of the synagogue relates to this as well; see Tur, O.H., end of 671, and the *Beit Yosef* there, citing the *Terumat ha-Deshen*, siman 104.
14. *Seder Hilkhot Hannukah*, p. 10.
15. Ed. Auerbach, vol. 2, pp. 20–21.
16. On Shabbat 21a, s.v. *i nami le-she'ura*.
17. She'ilta 26, ed. Mirsky, p. 174.
18. Chap. 3, p. 7a, and in shortened form in chap. 6, pp. 22b–23a.
19. Naso, siman 29, cited as "*yelammedenu Rabbenu.*"
20. See Shulhan Arukh, O.H. 674:1, in the *hagahah*, and compare his *Darkei Moshe he-Arokh* ad loc.
21. *Yehudei Kurdistan* (Jerusalem, 5708), p. 273.
22. Ed. Hamburger and Zimmer, vol. 1 (Jerusalem, 5748), siman 199, p. 240.
23. To be precise, it seems that the *shammash* was of wax, while the lamps themselves were filled with oil; see *Sefer Maharil*, ed. Spitzer, p. 403, n. *gimmel*: "He would draw the *shammash* up above all the other lights." The verb "draw" implies that a wax candle was used. This is stated explicitly in the variant readings there, n. *bet*: "and this was of wax." In contrast, *Sefer Maharil* says of the lamps themselves, that "he lit them [using] olive oil," and, again, the variant readings listed there, n. *dalet*: "which is the most expensive of all oils in the districts of the Rhine." See also R. Isaac Tyrnau, *Sefer ha-Minhagim*, ed. Spitzer, p. 143, n. 23, quoting *Or Zarua* II, siman 326, and *Sefer ha-Minhagim*,

p. 144, where wax candles are mentioned explicitly. See also *Minhagei R. Avraham Klausner*, ed. Dissen (Jerusalem, 5738), p. 63, n. *gimmel*, and *Beur Halakhah* to Shulhan Arukh, O.H. 671:*dalet*, s.v. *afilu* (and see *Darkei Moshe he-Arokh*, ibid., n. *alef*).

24. *Teshuvot, Pesaqim u-Minhagim*, ed. Kahana, I, p. 318, siman 605. See also *Ha-Minhagim de-Qehala Qadisha Vermaiza*, ed. Hamburg and Zimmer, vol. 1 (Jerusalem, 1988), p. 240.

25. No. 7 in Spitzer's edition of *Sefer Maharil*.

26. *Sefer Maharil*, ed. Spitzer, p. 403, variant readings n. *dalet*.

27. Vol. 5 (Jerusalem, 1988), p. 196, n. 20.

28. Hilkhot Hannukah 4:3.

29. Shabbat 21b, s.v. *veha-mehadderin*.

30. See *Kaf ha-Hayyim* 673, n. 18, quoting *Mahatzit ha-Sheqel*: "See the *TaZ*, who wrote in the name of the Maharal of Prague [see *Ner Mitzvah* 69b—D.S.], that it is forbidden to use wax candles, because their flame is like that of a torch," but, notes the Hida, "that is not the custom." The influential Sephardi decisor, the Hida, writes in a similar vein but in stronger language in his *Birkei Yosef* on O.H. 673, noting that *Elyah Rabba* also protested against this prohibition.

31. II, siman 35, cited in *Kaf ha-Hayyim* 673, n. 14.

32. At the beginning of Masekhet Tamid of his work, pp. 249a–b.

33. For purposes of comparison it is worthwhile to examine Pelc's tables of wages; a simple worker earned between 4 and 11½ groshen per day. On the economic status of Polish Jews in the period, see Y. Heilperin, *Beit Yisrael be-Polin*, vol. 1 (Jerusalem, 5708), p. 174, on the expansion of the Jewish middle and lower classes in this period, and the support provided them by the Rema and the *BaH*.

CHAPTER 24[1]
Kindling Hannukah Lights According to the Custom of the Jews of Persia

WE FIND THREE SEPARATE and distinct customs among Persian Jews in regard to the number of lights which are kindled each day of Hannukah. Some light one lamp on the first day and add an additional one on each of the succeeding days, according to the common custom, following Bet Hillel in Shabbat 21b. Another requires the lighting of three each day with the addition of one on each succeeding day; and the third begins with *eight* and adds *eight* more each additional night.[2]

The last custom is extremely puzzling; I have found nothing like it elsewhere, nor have I discerned its reason and origin. However, in regard to the second custom, which requires that one begin with three lights, there are sources which may elucidate and explain its rationale.

My friend and former student, Mr. Naftali Stern,

wrote an interesting article on the history of the *shammash* in halakhic literature.[3] He concludes, that there are two types of *shammash*. One is intended to light the Hannukah candles or lamps,[4] according to Rav's view that one may not use one Hannukah light to kindle another,[5] while the second serves as a source of permitted light, since "it is forbidden for us to use the Hannukah lights [for purposes] other [than] looking at them."

After examining the sources, Stern concluded that according to the Tur and the Shulhan Arukh (673) the two *shammashim* were used simultaneously—one for kindling the lights, and one to serve as a source of light. This explains the widespread use of Hanukkah menorahs with places for two additional candles, often raised above the level of the others, and often at opposite ends of the menorah. This positioning is not only for aesthetic reasons, but in accordance with the halakhic views mentioned above.[6]

It seems therefore that this view came to be expressed in the second custom of the Jews of Persia; they would kindle three lights, one for the mitzvah, one for the *shammash* used to kindle the actual Hannukah lights, and one for use as a source of light.

To carry the point somewhat further: this matter of two *shammashim* may explain a custom found among the Jews of Libya, where an additional light was kindled in the synagogues, along with the Hannukah lights and the *shammash*.[7] Perhaps there was more concern about the private use of the Hannukah lights in a public place than at home, where the extra light was not kindled. But more research is required.

Notes

1. *Minhagei Yisrael*, vol. 1, pp. 167-168, and vol. 5 (1995) pp. 49-54, 60-61. The whole of volume 5 is dedicated to Hannukah.
2. See *Nusah ha-Tefillah shel Yehudei Paras*, ed. Shlomo Tal (Jerusalem, 5741), pp. 189-190.
3. "Le-Toledot ha-Shammash shel Nerot Hannukah al pi Sifrut ha-Halakhah," *Sefer Yaakov Leslau* (Tel Aviv, 5745), pp. 344-357.
4. See *Sefer Ravyah*, siman 843, p. 576.
5. Shabbat 22a.
6. See *Catalogue of the Jewish Museum—London*, ed. R. D. Barnett (London, 1974), plate XCI, nos. 251, 252; plate LXXXVI, no. 266; and plate LXXX, no. 268 (with descriptions on pp. 50 and 52), and *Encyclopaedia Judaica*, vol. 7, col. 1298, no. 12; col. 1310, no. 35; col. 1314, no. 40, etc.
7. As described in A. Goldberg, *Qorot Lub ve-Yahadutah* . . . (Jerusalem, 5742), siman 97, p. 302, and see the editor's comment on p. 375, n. 12. Additional comments on this issue in *Minhagei Yisrael*, vol. 6.

CHAPTER 25[1]
The Parshiyot of Sheqalim, Zahkhor, and Hahodesh, According to the Custom of Eretz Israel

MISHNAH MEGILLAH 3:4 REPORTS on the order of the Four Parshiyot:

> [When] Rosh Hodesh Adar falls on the Sabbath, they read [Parashat] Sheqalim[2] [then]; [when] it falls during the week, it is read on the [Sabbath] before and interrupts [the Four Parshiyot for a week]. On the second [of the Sabbaths of the Four Parshiyot Parashat], Zakhor[3] is read; on the third [Parashat], Parah [the Red Heifer];[4] on the fourth, Parashat Hahodesh ["This month shall be for you"]; and on the fifth, they return to the [normal] order.[5]

216

Regarding the last stipulation the Bavli asks: "What [normal] order?" R. Ami says: "He returns to the [normal] order of Torah readings (*qeriot*)." R. Yirmiyah says: "He returns to the [normal] order of Haftarot." Said Abaye: "R. Ami's view is more likely, etc."

R. Ami's interpretation seems to reflect the plain sense of the Mishnah; only the special parashah of each of the Four Sabbaths was read; there was no other Torah reading. However, if so, a serious problem would have arisen, since several of these parashiyot are too short for a Sabbath Torah-reading, which must include at least twenty-one verses—three for each of the seven *aliyot*. Parashat Zakhor is only three verses in all; Parashat Sheqalim has only ten verses, and Parashat Hahodesh has twenty. How did they provide for the proper number of *aliyot* without any additional readings? This is especially, so given the fact that the adjacent passages in all these cases have little to do with the content of the special parashah. The *Turei Even*, who raises this question, suggests that each short parashah was repeated as many times as was necessary.

Support for this view comes from a Genizah fragment, published by Ezra Fleischer, which reflects the custom of Eretz Israel and depicts the manner of reading two of these four parshiyot according to that custom, Parashat Parah and Parashat Hahodesh.[6] This fragment contains directions for reading, and instructs (in Arabic): "He should take out one Torah scroll, and seven *aliyot* are read therein, from זאת חוקת התורה [Numbers 19:1] to ויט ישראל עליו

[Numbers 20:21]." The emphasis on "one Torah scroll" indicates that they did indeed *read only one parashah*, and did not read the regular parashah of the week—all this in accordance with R. Ami's interpretation.

This Genizah fragment contains forty-three verses, a length which is difficult to explain. Fleischer suggests that it was chosen in order "to make possible the division of the parashah into seven *aliyot*." However, as Fleischer himself notes, our custom, which is to end the reading of this parashah with verse 22 (והנפש הנוגעת תטמא עד הערב)—a total of twenty-two verses—easily divides into seven *aliyot*. Thus there was no need to continue on for another twenty-one verses!

It seems to me that the additional twenty-one verses took the reading to the end of the Eretz Israel *seder*. As is well known, the "western" custom was to read the Torah in a triennial cycle, with much shorter *sedarim* than our, Babylonian ones. Although Genizah lists give the end of the *seder* as Numbers 20:14,[7] and not 20:21, there is evidence from Eretz Israel midrashim that the latter was the end of the *seder*, at least according to one tradition.[8] In addition, "double *nuns*" appear after 20:21 in two Syrian Torah scrolls in the Sassoon collection—*nuns* which serve to indicate the beginning of a new *seder*.[9] It would seem, therefore, that this Genizah fragment indicates the reading of the entire *seder*, with seven *aliyot*.

How was the maftir handled? Did they repeat several verses at the end of the reading, as is the usual custom? Or, did they repeat the entire parashah another time, or did they do something else? The author's comments to the next parashah—Parashat Hahodesh—may give us a hint. After indicating that the reading should contain Exodus 12:1–29, with seven *aliyot*, the fragment continues: "and he should read again from החדש הזה until תקחו," i.e., Exodus 12:1–5. Now, Fleischer comments that according to our custom the reading ends with 12:20 (בכל מושבותיכם תאכלו מצות), and so the parashah contains only twenty verses—one short of the twenty-one needed for seven *aliyot*.[10] In order to provide for seven *aliyot*, the Genizah fragment has the reading continue for another nine verses, but that is eight more than necessary!

Once again the answer is that the reading continued to the end of the Eretz Israel *seder*, following the triennial division of *sedarim*. As far as the question of the maftir is concerned, however, the hint comes with the fragment's instruction to repeat 12:1–5. First seven *aliyot* covered the entire parashah to the additional nine verses, and then, doubling back to the beginning of the parashah, the first five verses were read, in order to emphasize that this was Parashat Hahodesh.[11]

We find the same practice in Babylonia, as noted in Megillah 30a, but in regard to the Babylonian division into *sedarim*. "[When Parashat Sheqalim] falls [on the Sabbath of] Ki Tissa itself, R. Isaac Napaha says: Six[12] read from (הכיור) ועשית את until ויקהל, and one reads from כי תשא until ועשית." That is, we read the *sedra* of Ki Tissa, excluding the first parashah, that of Sheqalim, and then return to the beginning and read Parashat Sheqalim at the end. To this, Abaye objects, that people will say that we are reading backwards. Instead, Abaye suggests that *all* of Ki Tissa is read, and then we repeat the parashah of Sheqalim once again. The Gemara then quotes a baraita which supports this view.

We may assume that a similar practice was employed in Eretz Israel. First, they read the entire *seder* (Numbers 19:1–20:21), divided into seven *aliyot*, and then, repeated 19:1–20 as the maftir.

If this is correct, we may reconstruct the reading of Parashat Zakhor, even though it is not preserved in this Genizah fragment. This parashah contains only three verses, Deuteronomy 25:17–19, and happens to come at the very end of an Eretz Israel triennial *seder*.[13] The *seder* begins with Deuteronomy 24:19 and includes twenty-three verses, enough for seven *aliyot*. It seems that they read the entire *seder* and then repeated the last three verses as a maftir, thus indicating the special nature of the Sabbath, Parashat Zakhor.

Thus from the evidence it seems, that the suggestion of the *Turei Even* and other Aharonim, that the custom of Eretz Israel was merely to repeat the parashah seven times, is not borne out. Instead, they read from the beginning of the *seder*, and repeated the last three verses as Parashat Zakhor only once.

ADDENDUM
The Eretz Israel Torah Reading of the Tokhahah of Vayikra[14]
Mishnah Megillah 3:4 teaches: "We do not interrupt [the

reading of] the Curses of Leviticus" (= Leviticus 26:3–45).
R. Yose explains this on the basis of Proverbs 3:11: "Do
not reject God's reproof, O my son, [and do not abhor
His rebuke]," while Resh Laqish suggests that we do not
recite a *berakhah* over [reports or threats of] punishment.[15] Rather, he suggests, the reading begins a verse
before and ends a verse after.[16]

Masekhet Soferim 12:1 gives yet another reason.
"Said R. Hiyya b. Gamda: Why? Because it is written,
'Do not abhor (תקוץ) His rebuke'—Do not make His
rebuke [into separate] pieces (קוצים קוצים)."[17] That is, do
not break the Tokhahah into separate parshiyot.

I do not want to enter into the complexities of this
short sugya, as discussed by Aharonim and scholars, in
connection with its various (partial) parallels elsewhere,[18] but rather to examine one particular point.

This is all more easily understood against the background of the Eretz Israel custom of a triennial cycle.
According to this cycle, the *seder* in which the Tokhahah is
located begins with Leviticus 26:3 and ends with 26:46—a
total of forty-four verses, twenty-nine of which belong to
the Tokhahah (verses 14–44).[19] As a result, therefore, there
are eleven verses before the Tokhahah, and three after it;
the last three verses are thus the seventh *aliyah*, the
Tokhahah itself is the sixth, and the eleven verses before it
must be divided into five *aliyot*. It would, of course, have
been easier to divide the entire forty-four verses into
seven *aliyot*, but the Halakhah prohibits dividing the
Tokhahah into separate parshiyot—קוצין קוצין.

221

The only way to produce five *aliyot* from the eleven verses preceding the Tokhahah is by repeating the last verse of each preceding *aliyah*, as follows:

Rishon: Leviticus 26:3, 4, 5
Sheni: Leviticus 26: 5, 6, 7
Shelishi: Leviticus 26: 7, 8, 9
Revi'i: Leviticus 26: 9, 10, 11
Hamishi: Leviticus 26: 11, 12, 13

Now, as for the Babylonian sugya cited above, that we begin with the verse before and end with the verse after,[20] the sixth *aliyah* would repeat the last verse of Hamishi, and the seventh the last verse of Shishi.

Shishi (Tokhahah): Leviticus 26:13 + 14–43 + 44
Shevi'i: Leviticus 26:44–46.

Here then, is the pattern of all the *aliyot*, taking all the halakhic problems we have raised into account.[21]

We find a similar situation in regard to the Anshe Maamad, as explained in Mishnah Taanit 4:3.[22]

Notes
  1. *Minhagei Yisrael*, vol. 1, pp. 88–91, and vol. 2, p. 264.
  2. Exodus 30:12–16, to remind people of the half-shekels donated for the Temple.
  3. Deuteronomy 25:17–19, to prepare for Purim, since Haman was descended from King Agag of Amalek.
  4. Numbers 19, to emphasize the importance of ritual purity before Passover.

5. Exodus 12, in preparation for Passover.
6. See Ezra Fleischer, *Tefillah u-Minhagei Tefillah Eretz Yisraeli-yim bi-Tequfat ha-Genizah* (Jerusalem, 5748), pp. 303–304.
7. As is indicated in the Koren Tanakh, and see N. Fried's article in *Tagim* 1 (1969), and the list on p. 68, as well as his description on p. 63. After the publication of this chapter in Hebrew, Uri Kellerman of Haifa referred me to the divisions in *Piyyutei Yannai*, ed. Z. M. Rabinowitz (Tel Aviv, 5745–47), siman 119, vol. 2, pp. 81 f., siman 53, vol. 1, pp. 296 f., and siman 158, vol. 2, pp. 171 f. My thanks to him for this and other comments.
8. See Fried, pp. 64–65. The evidence comes from various versions of Midrash Tanhuma and Midrash ha-Gadol.
9. See Fried, pp. 66–67.
10. See Fleischer, n. 51.
11. As Fleischer notes, n. 52.
12. This is according to the view that maftir is one of the seven *aliyot*, as was the custom in Yemen; see R. D. Sassoon, *Hatzofeh le-Hokhmat Yisrael* 1 (5684): 309–311, 316.
13. See Koren Tanakh, and M. Luban, "The Triennial Cycle" (diss., Yeshiva University, 1973), p. 160.
14. *Minhagei Yisrael*, vol. 2, pp. 264–267.
15. Compare Soferim 12:1, ed. Higger, p. 225: "Said R. Levi: The Holy One, blessed be He, says: 'It is not proper that I be blessed while My children are being cursed.' "
16. So in the Munich manuscript and the Ran; see *Diqduqei Soferim* there, *bet*. See also Tosafot there, s.v *mathil*, where they read, with most manuscripts: מתחיל בפסוק שלפניהם— without the word אחד. They understand the word *pasuq* as not necessarily referring to a verse, but perhaps to parashah, since we do not start with less than three verses before. However, this is all according to our custom, following the Babylonian annual cycle. According to the Eretz Israel triennial cycle, the word אחד, "one," is exact.

17. See ed. Higger, p. 224. Prof. M. Greenberg has drawn my attention to the fact that קיצין is the Samaritan term for parshiyot. I turned to Prof. Z. Ben Haim, the acknowledged expert on these matters, and he referred me to his edition of *Memar Marka* (Jerusalem, 1988), p. 345, n. 5, where he gives the singular as קצה and the plural as קצין; and see p. 355, n. 4, as well as the remarks of R. E. S. Rosenthal in *Sefer ha-Yovel le-Shai Agnon* (Ramat Gan, 5718), p. 300, on קוצין in Yerushalmi; see Yerushalmi Yoma 3:8 (74b), and Deuteronomy Rabba, beginning of chap. 4.

18. For now see R. Zevi Kohen, *Bein Pesah li-Shavuot* (5744), pp. 126 f., esp. n. 69, where he brings a wealth of sources from the Aharonim. The structure of the sugya is difficult, and I hope to return to this topic elsewhere. As for the parallels, see Higger's notes in his edition of Masekhet Soferim, p. 224, n. to l. 2, and see R. A. Zimmer, *Sinai* 68 (1971): 164, and R. S. Mirsky in *Talpiot* 3 (1947): 133–137.

19. See Y. Joel, *Kiryat Sefer* 38 (1963): 131, and J. Mann, *The Bible as Read and Preached in the Old Synagogue*, 2nd ed. (New York, 1971), vol. 2, p. 147. See the note of I. Sonne there, p. 173, n. 194, though his remarks are not convincing.

20. This halakhah, however, brings another problem in its wake: the verse before the Tokhahah (verse 13) immediately precedes a Masoretic parashah, and, according to Megillah 22a, "we do not leave less than three verses before [the end of] parashah [as an *aliyah*]." This halakhah violates this rule, presumably intentionally. The matter still requires qualification.

21. But see the last note.

    As far as the Tokhahah in Deuteronomy is concerned, however, there is no problem, since the Eretz Israel *seder* (*seder* 22) comprises Deuteronomy 28:1–29:8, while the Tokhahah itself takes up 28:15–68. Thus there are fourteen verses before the Tokhahah and nineteen after it. Deuteronomy 28:1–14 will easily accommodate four *aliyot*, the Tokhahah, 28:(14+)15–68(+69), if we add a verse before and after, is the fifth *aliyah*, and Deuteronomy 29:1–9 can certainly provide another two *aliyot*, Shishi and Shevi'i.

22. See Joel's comment in *Kiryat Sefer* (above, n. 18), p. 129, that there are *sedarim* which do not contain twenty-one verses (7 x 3), and they required similar repetitions. However, Prof. Ezra Fleischer has kindly written to me regarding this matter. "As I read [your article] I was concerned as to whether you were not exaggerating a bit . . . in regard to the fixity which you attribute to the length of the *sedarim* in Eretz Israel, and the exact beginning and end of each. It seems to me that we should not assume such exactitude in ancient times; indeed, the lengths to which you must go [in devising *aliyot*] for the *seder* which includes the Tokhahah will demonstrate that this is so. Whether we may with assurance assume that the triennial cycle was in effect in the time of the Mishnah is also now open to doubt. Indeed, it may be that the very fact that the Tokhahah was not to be interrupted demonstrates that the *sedarim* were actually quite long!"

However, my assumption that the triennial cycle was in effect at this time is strengthened by the indications that verses which end a *seder* open the Torah reading of the next one, as maintained in the important article by Yosef Ofer in *Tarbiz* 58 (1989); see pp. 163–165, 171.